Blue Collar Intellectuals

Blue Collar Intellectuals

When the Enlightened and the Everyman Elevated America

Daniel J. Flynn

Wilmington, Delaware

Chapter 1, "The Apostate Historians," appeared in abbreviated
form as "The Epic of the Durants," *National Review*, October
5, 2009.

Library of Congress Cataloging-in-Publication Data

Flynn, Daniel J.
    Blue collar intellectuals : when the enlightened and the
    everyman elevated America / by Daniel J. Flynn.
    p. cm.
    Includes bibliographical references and index.
    ISBN 978-1-61017-020-8

1. Intellectuals—United States—History—20th century. 2.
Blue collar workers—United States—History—20th century.
3. Reading—United States—History—20th century. I. Title.

HM728.F58 2011
305.5'5209730904—dc23
                                                2011033480

ISI Books
Intercollegiate Studies Institute
3901 Centerville Road
Wilmington, DE 19807-1938
www.isibooks.org

Manufactured in the United States of America

Contents

Blue Collar Intellectuals

Introduction

Blue Collar Intellectuals

Stupid is the new smart.

Consider the nostrums of the digital era. "Video gaming is just a new form of literacy."[1] "Reality shows . . . challenge our emotional intelligence."[2] "Who cares if Johnny can't read? The value of books is overstated."[3] "If you're not on MySpace, you don't exist."[4] Watching cartoons is "a kind of mental calisthenics" for small children.[5] "The truth is, we need multitasking as much as we need air."[6]

Translation?

World of Warcraft is not altogether different from *The Canterbury Tales*. Vicarious existence through reality television contestants enables us to enjoy healthier interactions with real people. Ignorance is underrated. Living is interacting through online intermediaries. Let your television babysit your kids. Attention deficit disorder is strength, not malady.

Welcome to Idiotville, population seven billion.

The Invasiveness of Stupidity

Pop culture is a wasteland.

The strange paradox of television is that viewing options have decreased even as the number of channels has dramatically increased. Viewers have their choice of hundreds of stations devoted to reality television, celebrity gossip, *Faces of Death*–lite-style home-video shows, and envy-inspiring vignettes on how wealthy people live. Worse still is television's invasiveness. Standing in the supermarket checkout line, waiting in the airport terminal, pumping gas at the service station, standing on the train, sitting in the backseat—there is no escape. People are afraid to be alone with their thoughts.

The newsstand is increasingly indecipherable from the supermarket checkout aisle. Celebrity news and shark attacks pass for what matters. Even political coverage resembles a dressed-up version of high-school gossip: He's popular/she's not. Can you believe that he is sleeping with her? Fight! Did you hear the outrageous thing he said? Something important generates interest only when reduced to its most trivial aspect. Declining readership has queerly motivated newspaper and magazine editors to race to the bottom to capture "readers" who don't read by dumbing down content and dramatically shaving word counts. All this has left Susan Jacoby to quip in *The Age of American Unreason*, "It is only a matter of time before a publication markets itself as 'The Magazine for People Who Hate to Read.'"[7]

The cultural rot is especially visible on the silver screen, which advertises Hollywood's lack of creativity by green-lighting sequels, remaking old movies, and providing cinematic treatments of long-canceled television shows. All mediocre movies are destined to be remade as even worse movies. What got red-lighted because *The A-Team*, *Herbie Fully Loaded*, *The Green Hornet*, and *The Day the Earth Stood Still* got green-lighted? The success of one 3-D movie unleashes a barrage of 3-D movies. An industry made on creativity persists on copycatism.

In popular music, the visual bizarrely trumps the audio. No amount of studio wizardry can make Miley Cyrus, Britney Spears, or Katy Perry sound like Aretha Franklin, Kate Smith, or Mama Cass. Of greater consequence, no amount of airbrushing can make today's Aretha Franklins, Kate Smiths, or Mama Casses look like Miley Cyrus, Britney Spears, or Katy Perry—who clearly possess the most important prerequisite to a successful career as a recording artist. Are fat, ugly, and old people necessarily bad singers too?

The World Wide Web has ironically made life more insular. The popularity of social networking sites extends the clique's reach online; Twitter broadcasts the inane musings of one's favorite celebrities in 140 characters or less; and BlackBerries allow for the illusion of keeping in touch by staying beyond the touch of friends and loved ones. The Staten Island teenager who fell down a manhole while texting, the Sacramento high school senior who sent and received 300,000 texts in one month, and the Pennsylvania woman who obliviously texted her way into a mall fountain are signs of the times.[8]

People are too lost in the virtual life. They have lost track of how to live the real life. New amusements have not made old distractions obsolete. Americans spend more than two and a half hours every weekday watching television. The figure has *risen* since the advent of the digital age. By way of comparison, Americans spend about twenty minutes per weekday reading and about fifteen minutes "relaxing/thinking."[9] How we spend our leisure time is largely a waste of time.

"I Don't Read Books"

Pop culture, of course, is not high culture. It has always appealed to the lowest common denominator. But reaching the lowest common denominator has never required pop culture to go so low. More disturbing, and injurious, is the go-along-to-get-along mentality of institutions ostensibly committed to cultural betterment. Libraries, schools, and museums rationalize assaults on culture as defenses of it.

At tony Cushing Academy in western Massachusetts, $40,000 in tuition doesn't even get you a library anymore. "When I look at books, I see an outdated technology, like scrolls before books," the prep school's headmaster notes, adding, "This isn't *Fahrenheit 451*." It is, and *1984*, too. In the place of twenty thousand discarded books, the school spent $500,000 on an Orwellian "learning center" complete with three giant flat-screen televisions and a cappuccino machine. School officials guessed that only a few dozen books had been checked out at any one time. "When you hear the word 'library,' you think of books," one student explained to the *Boston Globe*, "but very few students actually read them."[10] The solution to this problem, so obvious to the administrators at this preparatory school, was to abolish books.

"I don't read books," a Rhodes Scholar and former student body president of Florida State University explains. "Sitting down and going through a book from cover to cover doesn't make sense." He Googles his way to the answer. A Duke University professor of literature candidly confesses, "I can't get my students to read whole books anymore."[11] These aren't dropouts scorning literacy but rather the young adults touted as the best and the brightest. Intelligent people are using reason to rationalize intellectual laziness as progress and ridiculing time-tested methods of acquiring knowledge, wisdom, and understanding as outdated.

Much of K–12 schooling involves educating for a standardized test, superficial learning that does to the mind what Botox, steroids, and plastic surgery do to the body. The type of education predominant in college is professional training that prepares cogs to fit into the economy rather than liberally educated citizens ready for the responsibilities of freedom. Institutions that shun broad knowledge graduate shallow people with narrow interests.

Quest for Learning is a public school in Manhattan where students play video games, blog, create podcasts, film YouTube-style videos, and partake in other digital activities that young people overdose on outside of the classroom. They also call their teachers by their first names, refer to their school as a "possibility space," and forgo traditional lettered grades for "pre-novice," "novice," "apprentice," "senior," and "master." Crassly mixing philanthropy with business, the Bill and Melinda Gates Foundation helps fund the school. Teacher Al Doyle calls spelling "outmoded," says that podcasting is "as valid as writing an essay," and regards memorization as irrelevant in light of search engines. "Handwriting?" Doyle remarks. "That's a 20th-century skill." It was surprisingly unsurprising when the *New York Times Magazine* said of the school's executive director, "Until a few years ago she knew little about educational pedagogy and was instead immersed in doing things like converting an ice-cream truck into a mobile karaoke unit that traveled around San Jose, Calif., with a man dressed as a squirrel dispensing free frozen treats and encouraging city residents to pick up a microphone and belt out tunes."[12]

"In the 21st century, libraries are about much more than books!" the American Library Association boasts in conjunction with its National Gaming Day, "the largest, simultaneous national video game tournament ever held!"[13] In the midst of branch closings and budget cuts, public libraries have acquired a new product to lend: video games. "The literacy aspect is huge," maintains Linda Braun of the Young Adult Library Services Association. "Many video games have books related to them. And there is a lot of reading that goes on with actual game play."[14] In addition to lending discs, libraries host massive video-game tournaments and feature on-site consoles allowing patrons to play. "A library is no longer *just* a place for books," argues Ryan Donovan, a public librarian in Manhattan. He says that gaming involves "a high degree of literacy and problem solving skills" and will "hopefully attract a new audience to NYPL [New York Public Library]."[15] "Video games have evolved," explains Allen Kesinger, organizer of the National Gaming Day at a library in Southern California. "They have become a medium to deliver sophisticated, emotionally charged stories." He claims that "this strong focus on narrative" will help libraries "attract hesitant readers."[16] It is an open question whether games will serve as a gateway to books, as some librarians hope. Settled is their role transforming libraries from centers of education to centers of amusement, from quiet sanctuaries in a noisy world to extensions of that high-decibel environment in which "shh" is the only verboten sound.

Science writer Steven Johnson, author of a book called *Everything Bad Is Good for You*, lauds the virtues of television zombies and mesmerized gamers: "Parents can sometimes be appalled at the hypnotic effect that television has on toddlers; they see their otherwise vibrant and active children gazing silently, mouth agape at the screen, and they assume the worst: the television is turning their child into a zombie. The same feeling arrives a few years later, when they see their grade-schoolers navigating through a video game world, oblivious to the reality that surrounds them. But these expressions are not signs of mental atrophy. They're signs of *focus*."[17]

It is later than you think.

The Historians, the Educator, the Economist, the Philosopher, and the Storyteller

It wasn't always so.

For much of the twentieth century, there was a concerted effort among intellectuals to spread knowledge and wisdom far and wide. Correspondingly, many regular people took full advantage of the great educational effort. Rather than mind-numbing amusements invading places of learning, learning invaded the leisure space. Blue-collar intellectuals were those most fervently dedicated to the idea of a well-rounded, educated citizenry.

A blue-collar intellectual is a thinker who hails from a working-class background, and whose intellectual work targets, in part or whole, a mass audience. Given that blue-collar intellectuals benefited by such outreach efforts when they were more blue collar than intellectual, it is hardly surprising that they would lead such efforts when they found themselves in positions to do so.

This book focuses on a half dozen blue-collar intellectuals:

- Before Will and Ariel Durant partnered to write books, they joined in a scandalous marriage uniting a teacher with his child-bride student. Will, a seminarian excommunicated from his church, and Ariel, a pariah within her immigrant family for marrying a gentile, appeared destined for divorce. But the partnership yielded appearances on best-seller lists from the 1920s until the 1970s, and a Pulitzer Prize in 1968. Despite serving as the de facto professors of world history to millions, the Durants have strangely escaped the interest of actual professors of history.
- Mortimer Adler, an Ivy League Ph.D. who held neither high school nor college degree, fittingly launched the most successful adult education program in history, the Great Books Movement. As much a salesman as a scholar, Adler successfully marketed ancient texts to television-age America.
- Milton Friedman received state scholarships to Rutgers, New Deal employment, and government research grants. Then the pragmatic libertarian became the twentieth century's most effective exponent of the free market, winning the Nobel Prize in 1976. Whereas the other giant of twentieth-century economics, John Maynard Keynes, the scion of a famous economist, was educated at Eton and

Cambridge and cavorted in an aristocratic bisexual clique, Friedman was the progeny of Jewish immigrants whose Rahway, New Jersey, home doubled as a sweatshop.

• Dubbed "Ike's favorite author," Eric Hoffer captured America's imagination in two prime-time CBS specials and left an indelible mark on political discourse through his landmark book, *The True Believer.* He was an intellectual everyman who migrated from skid row anonymity to Rose Garden chats with the president. Though readers continue to consult the unschooled but well-educated longshoreman philosopher, writers have overlooked one of the twentieth century's most fascinating lives.

• So destitute that he shared the same cot with his brother into adulthood, so awkward that even dorks brushed him off, Ray Bradbury elevated his lowly finances and meager social status by selling five million copies of *Fahrenheit 451*, penning teleplays for *Alfred Hitchcock Presents*, *The Twilight Zone*, and ultimately his own *Ray Bradbury Theater*, and placing stories in *Mademoiselle*, *Harper's*, *Playboy*, and *The New Yorker*. In the process of lifting himself up, the "poet of the pulps" elevated not only his readers but heretofore marginal genres such as science fiction as well.

Blue-collar intellectuals spoke to educated laymen without talking down to them. In the process, they uplifted the masses and rescued ideas from the academic ghetto. Such sins are not easily forgiven.

The Great Uplift

A specific time and place gave rise to blue-collar intellectuals. Twentieth-century America witnessed a
democratization of education unparalleled in human
history. Aided by cheap printing, technological inno-
vations in communications, and a wider dissemination
of wealth, strivers bettered themselves through the G.I.
Bill and adult continuing education programs; National
Educational Television and university-of-the-air style
radio programs; Little Blue Books, the Book-of-the-
Month Club, the advent of paperbacks, and broad "outline" books; popular middlebrow magazines such as
Saturday Review and *The New Yorker*; and social out-
lets such as community book clubs, museums, Andrew
Carnegie–funded libraries, and Great Books programs.

In America, where yesterday's poor became today's
rich, money became a wanting benchmark to distin-
guish class. Education supplanted money as a measure
of status. In 1949, a prophetic Russell Lynes foresaw,
"What we are headed for is a sort of social structure in
which the highbrows are the elite, the middlebrows are
the bourgeoisie, and the lowbrows are *hoi polloi.*" Blue-
collar intellectuals proved as unsettling to the intellectual elite as the nouveau riche had been to old money.
Worse still, they replicated their numbers through
evangelization. Lynes further observed of the highbrow, "The fact that nowadays everyone has access to
culture through schools and colleges, through the press,
radio, and museums, disturbs him deeply; for it tends
to blur the distinctions between those who are serious
and those who are frivolous."[18] How dare people who

mistook their salad fork for their dinner fork lecture us on culture?

Rather than welcoming the massive attempt at intellectual uplift, intellectuals heaped scorn upon it. They dismissed the democratization of knowledge and wisdom as an invasion of their turf by undesirables. Established intellectuals adopted a vocabulary to demarcate intellectual class—"lowbrow," "middlebrow," "highbrow"—with "middlebrow" becoming a slur akin to "bourgeois" in the Marxian vernacular.

Dwight Macdonald, for instance, held that "there is something damnably American about Midcult."[19] Virginia Woolf threatened, "If any human being, man, woman, dog, cat or half-crushed worm dares call me 'middlebrow' I will take my pen and stab him, dead."[20] Paul Fussell sniffed in his book *Class*, "It is in the home of middle-class dwelling that you're likely to spot the fifty-four-volume set of the Great Books, together with the half-witted two-volume Syntopicon, because the middles, the great audience for how-to books, believe in authorities."[21]

Highbrows believe in guides, too, only their guides, strangely enough, are the dreaded middlebrows. Highbrows instinctively do the opposite of what middlebrows are doing. So down from the shelves came the classics and up went unread works by Derrida, Barthes, Habermas, and other lords of indecipherability that, if strategically placed on a shelf in the living room, advertised their owners as bona fide intellectuals.

Instead of engaging the mass culture, intellectuals visibly flee from it. The most convincing demonstration of the pseudointellectualism of large parts of academia came from physicist Alan Sokal's success placing a jargon-filled article in the "scholarly" journal *Social Text* advancing such patently ridiculous ideas as equality in mathematics owing a debt to feminism. "Would a leading North America journal of cultural studies," Sokal wondered, "publish an article liberally salted with nonsense if (a) it sounded good and (b) it flattered the editors' ideological preconceptions?"[22] The cultural guardians had answered "yes." The ivory tower has become a tower of babble.

The insider language used in journals and at conferences, the adversarial politics of alienation, and even the fashion (observe professors in winter dress late during the spring semester) make it evident that academics take pains to appear separate from the surrounding culture. Accomplishment does not define elites; mannerisms, jargon, and appearances do. Never has elitism been so mediocre.

Events have forced a reassessment of the middlebrow's quest for betterment. The domination of television by people named Snooki and Dog and Omarosa, and the transformation of the local library from a repository of books to a center for cruising sex over the Internet, tends to spark such epiphanies. Highbrows have begun having second thoughts about the climbers they formerly denigrated.

"I look back on the middlebrow with affection, gratitude, and regret rather than condescension not because the Book-of-the-Month Club brought works of genius into my life but because the monthly pronouncements of its reviewers were one of the many sources that encouraged me to seek a wider world," Susan Jacoby reminisces. "That people should aspire to read and think about great books, or even aspire to being thought of as the sort of person who reads great books, is not a bad thing for a society."[23]

There was a massive demand for blue-collar intellectuals throughout much of the twentieth century because there was a massive demand for intellectual betterment. There isn't a massive supply of blue-collar intellectuals today because the enlightened do not feel a vocational pull to reach out to the everyman and the everyman expresses little demand for intellectual betterment. There is not even a consensus that reading means intellectual betterment, let alone about what we should be reading. A society in which it is maladaptive to discuss *The Nicomachean Ethics*, *Othello*, and *The Federalist Papers* is a maladaptive society. The cultural common denominators of the past aren't so common anymore. One can reference *The Simpsons* or *Anchorman* or an Eminem lyric with the understanding that an educated audience will know what one is talking about. Try doing that with *The Odyssey* or *Moby Dick* even. What it means to be an educated person has changed for the worse.

The intellectual and the everyman suffer when the life of the mind is deemed the exclusive domain of intellectuals. Segregated from society by academic jargon, minute specialization, and outright snobbery, intellectuals descend into a ghetto of unintelligible babble remote from mass society. Similarly, today's middlebrow becomes yesterday's lowbrow when *Tool Academy*, *Grand Theft Auto IV*, cage fighting, and Internet pornography crowd out the pursuit of higher things within mass culture. Comfortable in the sensate cesspool demanding of neither the intellect nor the soul, the everyman makes no effort to ascend from the muck. Grateful for the status separation, the intellectual does nothing to raise the mass and everything to extenuate his privileged apartness.

"We are increasingly ignorant, but we do not know enough to be properly ashamed," lamented W. A. Pannapacker, writing in the *Chronicle of Higher Education.* "If we are determined to get on in life, we believe it will not have anything to do with our ability to reference Machiavelli or Adam Smith at the office Christmas party. The rejection of the Great Books signifies a declining belief in the value of anything without a direct practical application, combined with the triumph of a passive entertainment."[24]

Regular people can still find smart if they look hard enough. This is a book about a moment when smart looked hard enough to find regular people.

The Apostate Historians

How an Excommunicated
"Cradle Robber" and His Anarchist
Child Bride Made History

More than eight decades after they started to write the history of the world, Will and Ariel Durant's project seems more absurd than ever. Two feet of books, uninterested in the times and nation of its readers, hardly make for a rush on Barnes and Noble's checkout lines. But during its four-decade run, *The Story of Civilization*'s volumes regularly invaded best-seller lists. The Durants, who won both a Pulitzer Prize and the Presidential Medal of Freedom, bridged the chasm that separates scholars and laymen.

The last entry in their eleven-volume series, *The Age of Napoleon*, hit the *New York Times* best-seller list in 1975.[1] Six years later, both Will and Ariel Durant passed away. They died within a fortnight of each other, which seemed fitting. They lived, labored, and loved for so long in such close quarters that denying one the other might have struck some as evidence of a sadistic God.

When they were married sixty-eight years earlier, nothing would have seemed more far-fetched than the prosperous union that followed. Before Will and Ariel Durant's names became inseparable on dust jackets, they had been joined in scandal.

Losing Faith

Ariel's meeting Will was a case of divine nonintervention.

After teaching at Seton Hall during 1907–8 school year, blue-collar bookworm Durant pleased his Catholic parents and advanced his education by entering the New Jersey school's seminary. He found Baruch Spinoza in the stacks. He lost God. Enticed to remain by a priest confident in his return to the flock, by his pay as a teacher at the college, and by dreams of reconciling Catholicism and socialism, Durant lasted almost two years as an agnostic seminarian. Conscience compelled him to quit.

Floating out of one sect, he floated into another. Coaxed by a five-dollar honorarium to speak at the Francisco Ferrer Association, the struggling substitute teacher lectured true-believing New York City anarchists on the origins of religion. As if a lecture on homosexuality, masturbation, and birth control wasn't offensive enough to the church fathers, Durant, billed as a Seton Hall professor, added his two cents on the role of phallic symbols in religion. The reaction was swift and severe. In January 1912, Monsignor James Mooney, who had mentored Durant in the faith, pronounced on the front page of the *Newark Evening News* that the lecture represented "an apostasy from the Catholic religion and [should] entail excommunication."[2] His hero Spinoza's excommunication had merely provoked a knife attack. Durant's devastated his mother.

The fireworks surrounding Durant's split from the old faith would eventually be drowned out by a dynamite departure from the new faith. But initially, the nonconformism that made Durant anathema to Catholics made him attractive to anarchists. In the first of life's many transitions, Will Durant traded the discipline of Seton Hall for the latitudinarianism of the Ferrer School, which disposed of grades, detention, compulsory lessons, tardiness, and even the notion of *the* teacher. Durant's students skipped rope inside the classroom and pelted him with snowballs outside of it.[3] Will served as the principal/teacher/everything of the anarchist school; Ariel was its student most committed to classroom anarchy.

The teacher, too, took advantage of the peculiar rules (or lack thereof). Durant confessed to his bosses in 1913 that though "my feelings for Ariel were those of fatherly or brotherly interest; I say now that I love the girl."[4] At fourteen, that precocious, buxom girl had attended one of Durant's lectures on free love, posed nude for a Ferrer Center art class, and developed the habit of liberally dispensing hugs and kisses.[5] But this doesn't erase the fact that when student and teacher became attached, Ariel was still just fourteen. Durant tendered his resignation, which his overseers did their damnedest to rebuff. It was a school named for an executed Spanish anarchist, after all.

Departing after the 1912–13 school year, teacher married student, appropriately enough, that Halloween. The bride roller-skated from Harlem to City Hall, transportation slung over shoulder for the ceremony. The judge scolded the groom as a "cradle robber" and lectured to delay consummating the marriage until Ariel's sixteenth birthday.[6]

Though the teacher-student romance was, in Will's words, "the scandal of a season," the season did not last long.[7] A year after Durant's resignation, three anarchists transformed a Harlem tenement into an arsenal just blocks from the Ferrer School, where they had attended evening lectures *and* plotted terrorism. Pupils of the school Durant had overseen actually stood guard outside of the clandestine meetings.[8] Like three Weathermen across town fifty-six years later, the anarchist trio dismembered themselves instead of the intended targets of their bomb—John D. Rockefeller Jr. and the partygoers at his 1914 Fourth of July picnic. In *Transition,* his novelized autobiography, Durant falls asleep at ground zero—artistic license that *Time* magazine later confused for fact. Though the real Durant was in New Jersey at the time, it's worth noting that he was among those who facilitated the escape of a fourth conspirator who had been sleeping in the tenement when the explosion occurred.[9]

Like the Durants' intergenerational romance, the bombers hardly scandalized Ferrer School radicals. Planned Parenthood matriarch Margaret Sanger, her son a former Durant student, used the *Woman Rebel* to lionize Rockefeller's would-be assassins, proclaiming dynamite's "great value" and imploring radicals to "exult in every act of revolt against oppression." She published "A Defense of Assassination," which called for Rockefeller's murder. The *Woman Rebel,* suppressed; its editor, indicted—Sanger fled America.[10] Future Communist Party literary commissar Mike Gold penned a youthful ode lamenting that the bombers just "loved too much."[11]

Plot puppeteer Alexander Berkman, failed assassin of Andrew Carnegie's lieutenant Henry Clay Frick, failed again in orchestrating an industrialist's demise but succeeded this time in evading justice—even as he organized a demonstration that celebrated his puppets as martyrs.[12]

As Durant had lost the faith of his fathers, he now lost the faith of his comrades. "I came now to feel toward anarchism very much as I felt toward Catholicism: I could give it respect and sympathy even though I withheld belief," Will wrote in *Transition*. "But I bore from that moment a new sadness in my heart as I realized that I was fated, bit by bit and day by day, to lose my Utopian aspirations as I had lost, in younger days, my hope of immortality and heaven."[13] Those utopian illusions eroded further when he went on a European junket paid for by Alden Freeman, the sugar daddy of the Ferrer School. Just as Freeman's Standard Oil fortune had ironically helped bankroll a plot to kill a Rockefeller, his patronage of Durant's trip provided an ironic comeuppance, too. Seeing the basket-case states of postwar Europe made Durant pine for home rather than rail against it. "We had compared our country not with other nations of this earth," he wrote, "but with some perfect state which we had pictured in our dreams."[14] What do they know of America who only America know?

Although Durant reckoned himself a nonbelieving Christian after the loss of his faith, he embraced the socialist label for the duration despite airing views heretical to his political creed. Like the Seton Hall priests who had offered the seminarian employment after he confessed his disbelief, Freeman remained Durant's patron, sending him to graduate school at Columbia University to study philosophy.[15] People liked Will Durant even when he gave them reasons not to.

Columbia, radical breeding ground for Whitaker Chambers, Elizabeth Bentley, Corliss Lamont, and Mark Rudd, strangely had the opposite effect on the seminarian-turned-socialist. Durant's Freeman-funded study of philosophy sparked a realization that many of his political milieu's supposedly novel ideas had been tried and had failed too many times to count.[16]

A New Religion

He remained in that milieu but not of it. At Manhattan's Labor Temple, where twice weekly he imparted the wisdom of the ages to workingmen, passersby, and Greenwich Village denizens who could afford the twenty-five-cent tuition, Durant was dubbed a "one-man university."[17] Destined for Sunday sermonizing, the seminarian-turned-excommunicant delivered homilies at the Fourteenth Street and Second Avenue temple ironically announced in the *New York Times*'s church services listings.[18] Knowledge was his new religion, and he would spread the good news with a convert's fervor. Foreshadowing his boldness in writing the history of the world, and laying the groundwork for such a ridiculously ambitious project, the polymath lectured on "Montaigne," "Sophocles: Antigone," "The Nervous System," "Richard Wagner: Artist," "Recent Physics: Man and the Atom," and so on.[19]

If the quarter price was right for Durant's experiment in continuing education, then the nickels spent on Emanuel Haldeman-Julius's blue pamphlets bought a bargain. When the Kansas-based publisher wandered into the Labor Temple in 1922 to catch Durant's lecture on Plato, more than destiny seemed at work. Each one must have seen the other as a kindred spirit. Both men had flouted marital norms: Durant by taking a child bride, Haldeman-Julius by taking his wife's surname. More importantly, both men had been engaged in providing the masses an elite education. Whereas Durant lectured mass audiences on the history of philosophy, Haldeman-Julius published for the common man the "Little Blue Books," an ingenious series of staple-bound pocket primers on every subject imaginable. The pair stood at the ground floor of the democratization of education that characterized twentieth-century America.

Back in Girard, Kansas, where out of the ashes of the monster socialist weekly *Appeal to Reason* rose the Little Blue Books, Haldeman-Julius petitioned Durant to pen a fifteen-thousand-word monograph on Plato. Busy, Durant demurred. Persistent, Haldeman-Julius sent a check for $150. Like the Ferrer Association's $5 fee, it was an offer the young Ph.D. couldn't refuse. Another volume on Aristotle followed another check. Eleven Durant-authored Little Blue Books made their way into print between 1922 and 1925. By 1926, sales of Durant's primers—ultimately nearing two million copies—prompted the entrepreneurial socialist Haldeman-Julius to think of properly binding the collection between two hard covers. He commended Durant to twentysomething upstart bookmen Dick Simon and Max Schuster.[20]

While taking a freshman philosophy course at Columbia, Schuster had become fascinated with the lives of the philosophers. The future publisher suggested to his instructor, Walter Pitkin, that he write a book based on his biography-driven philosophy class.[21] Pitkin never seized the moment, but another Columbia philosopher, Will Durant, did so without Schuster's provocation. Schuster had not only devoured Durant's Little Blue Books but had read his Columbia dissertation as well.[22] The publishers believed in the product. More importantly, they believed in promotion.

The innovative pair poured exponentially more money into advertising than other firms, employed direct mail, offered special incentives to booksellers, and relied on gimmicks such as money-back guarantees to make Durant's book, *The Story of Philosophy*, a blockbuster.[23] A November 26, 1926, *New York Times* ad named sixty-six cities in which the firm's prized book ruled the best-seller list.[24] The advert essentially invited readers to come read what everybody else was reading. Two months later, another full-page S&S advertisement proclaimed that the massive success of a philosophy book revealed "a deep intellectual curiosity and an underlying seriousness that should certainly make us revise our opinion of ourselves as a nation composed largely of Main Street morons."[25]

The Story of Philosophy remained on the annual top-ten nonfiction best-seller list for four of the five years between 1926 and 1930, and was the single best-selling hardcover nonfiction book of 1927.[26] Durant established Simon and Schuster, heretofore known primarily for selling crossword-puzzle books, as publishing giants. And he provided himself the cash-register cachet to chart his own course.

Partners in Marriage, Partners in Scholarship

The commercial success of a book on Aristotle, Nietzsche, Spinoza, and other philosophers says as much about Durant's crowd-pleasing style as it does about the crowd. Long before *Guitar Hero,* Perez Hilton, and *MANswers,* the arms of the masses occasionally reached for something higher instead of dragging ever lower. Evidence suggests that Durant served as a gateway to rather than a mere summarizer of the classics. Joan Shelley Rubin points out in *The Making of Middlebrow Culture* that "the increase in sales of the Modern Library's philosophy titles in 1926 argues that Durant motivated some readers to delve into his sources."[27] So, too, does a letter to Durant from the New York Public Library noting a massive increase in patrons borrowing philosophical books in the wake of *The Story of Philosophy.*[28] Strangely, critics viewed Durant's project as part of the dumbing down of culture, as if it somehow sullied the greatest philosophers to encourage mechanics with dirty hands to read their books. As Durant put it, *The Story of Philosophy* was "disgracefully and unforgivably popular."[29] Snobs, not for the last time, looked down on an attempt at cultural uplift.

Durant defended the broad, accessible "outline" style of the day, best exemplified by H. G. Wells's comically ambitious and wildly popular two-volume *Outline of History.* The philosopher lamented that after the revolution of knowledge,

All that remained was the scientific specialist, who knew "more and more about less and less," and the philosophical speculator, who knew less and less about more and more. The specialist put on blinders to shut from his vision all the world but one little spot, to which he glued his nose. Perspective was lost. "Facts" replaced understanding; and knowledge, split into a thousand isolated fragments, no longer generated wisdom. Every science, and every branch of philosophy, developed a technical terminology intelligible only to its exclusive devotees; as men learned more about the world, they found themselves ever less capable of expressing to their educated fellow-men what it was that they had learned. The gap between life and knowledge grew wider and wider; those who governed could not understand those who thought, and those who wanted to know could not understand those who knew. In the midst of unprecedented learning popular ignorance flourished.[30]

The Durants filled the void. Their project sought to bring the education of the few to the many. Their lives exemplified the fruits of such an effort.

Born Chaya Kaufman in a Ukrainian Jewish ghetto, Ariel—whom Will nicknamed for the spirit in Shakespeare's *Tempest*—was briefly struck blind during passage from Old World to New. Temporary quarantine in Liverpool to deal with the mysterious malady resulted in her family's permanent quarantine from their possessions. With her family's luggage traveling to America without them, Ariel's hard-luck immigrant experience reads as a caricature.

Will's upbringing in a supersized family of ten conformed to Catholic stereotypes. His French-Canadian immigrant parents spoke French in the home. His factory-worker father never learned to read. When Will and Ariel married, the religious differences rather than the age gap scandalized family members.[31] What brought them together, and raised them from meager upbringings, was education. For Will, the Jesuits imparted knowledge and wisdom; for Ariel, Will did.

From where they came and to whom they directed their writings made the Durants the consummate blue-collar intellectuals. But by the late 1920s, Ariel's work as the proprietor of the Gypsy Tavern made her more blue collar than intellectual—even in a bohemian haunt barely escaping the Washington Square Arch's shadow. With Will buried in his books and Ariel behind her bar, the Durants reached a marital crossroads. "If we could only find a way in which each of us would enter more fully into the life of the other," Will wrote. He offered to go out semiweekly with his wife if she joined him in an intellectual partnership for the week's remaining days. Ariel gradually turned over her bar to relatives and joined Will in the project that would dominate their remaining half century. "Our love was renewed," Ariel recalled, "and our lives became one."[32]

The Durants embarked on their intellectual odyssey on the SS *Franconia*, which left New York on January 11, 1930, to explore such exotic locales as Algiers, Cairo, Nazareth, Bombay, Madras, Ceylon, Rangoon, Bangkok, Saigon, Canton, Shanghai, and Osaka. With *The Story of Philosophy*'s proceeds, the Durants paid $18,000 for two staterooms housing Will, Ariel, daughter Ethel, and two hundred books.[33]

The outline of *Our Oriental Heritage*, *The Story of Civilization*'s first entry, matched its author's travels.

Sections moved west to east. Chapters moved past to present. Will presented Ariel with chapter outlines, accompanied by notes, and Ariel organized Will's slips of paper into the relevant subheads on art, religion, war, and so on until they constituted a chapter. Even when wife joined husband on the book covers starting with 1961's *Age of Reason Begins,* Will remained writer while Ariel continued her multifarious roles as researcher, secretary, sounding board, and devil's advocate. "We estimate that an average chapter of the *Story* used some fifteen hundred slips, or about thirty thousand per volume; our attic rooms are bulging with the boxes of used slips," Ariel recalled in 1977. "All in all, the gathering of the material for Volume I (ignoring the gleanings made before 1929) took two years; the classification, one year; the writing and rewriting (in longhand), and the typing, two years; the printing, proofreading, and illustration, one year."[34] The weighty tome became a bestseller in New York, Chicago, San Francisco, Washington, Atlanta, New Orleans, and points beyond.[35] This pattern of telling the story of civilization, and of gracing the best-seller lists, repeated ten times.

The Durants' globe-trotting jaunts recurred with great frequency too. In 1932, the couple embarked on a trip wholly irrelevant to the content of *The Story of Civilization* but crucial to its critical reception. They spent nearly a month in Soviet Russia, which Will called a "gigantic prison." He became convinced that the Soviet "dictatorship of fanatics" had "allowed its people to starve by the thousands," "oppressed with unsurpassed barbarity men and women guilty of no other crime than the prosperity attendant upon enterprise, industry, intelligence, and thrift," and "deported or shot hundreds of thousands of men and women solely for political heresy and nonconformance."[36]

Durant attempted to sell his reflections on Russia to the day's leading magazines. *The Atlantic Monthly* and *Harper's* balked. It was the 1930s, and editors expected ideological tourists to dutifully return home with tales of heaven on earth. Durant described a place resembling a more sweltering afterlife destination. *The Saturday Evening Post,* offering $6,000 during the depths of the Depression for the four-part serial, rescued Durant's travel journals from the dustbin of a historian.[37]

Durant's reflections on the Soviet Union prompted Will Rogers to say, "He is just about our best writer on Russia. He is the most fearless writer that has been there."[38] But the intelligentsia did not share this view. The *Saturday Evening Post* serial enraged the Communists and fellow travelers who bullied writers in the 1930s. John Reed, Lincoln Steffens, and W. E. B. Du Bois had found heaven on earth there.[39] Why hadn't Will Durant?

Durant's political apostasy extended beyond criticizing the USSR. He also called out his fellow liberals for refusing to acknowledge reality. "Surely the time has come for the intellectuals, the liberals and the radicals of the world to speak out about this new slavery, to call it clearly and bluntly what it is," wrote Durant, who recalled his difficulty selling the article as much as his time in the Soviet Union. "For it can no longer be doubted that in this dictatorship of politicians is to be found every abuse which liberals and radicals have denounced in their own societies for generations."[40]

Despite a Simon and Schuster editor's warning that an unfavorable book about Soviet Russia would further alienate reviewers, a determined Durant bound his series in *The Tragedy of Russia* (1933).[41] This credentialed radical who upon news of the Bolshevik Revolution had proclaimed "Holy Russia" the "gentle Christ of the Nations" now played the Judas. His book, articles, and lectures on Russia, he discovered, "won me large audiences and many enemies."[42]

The Story of *The Story of Civilization*

To the Durants' "many enemies," the failure to extol the wonders of Soviet Russia was not the couple's only sin against intellectuals. The Durants' affront to academia's guild mentality was another. Will and Ariel were independent scholars unaffiliated with institutions of higher learning, and more infuriating was the fact that neither of America's first couple of history was a properly credentialed historian. It was bad enough that Will was an interloper from philosophy; Ariel hadn't even a college degree.

As independent scholars, the Durants rebelled against the approach of professional historians. They eschewed theory-driven history for people-driven history, microscopic specialization for broad synthesis, and the clique's jargon for the King's English. This irked scholars but pleased readers. *The Story of Civilization* extracted history from the academic ghetto whither it had retreated, opening the conversation about the past to all comers.

The Durants' style of cutting to the point, and the academic's manner of obscuring it, made them anathema to academicians who saw clarity as vice and not virtue. Their critics wrote to be cited. The Durants wrote to be read. *The Story of Civilization,* as critics praised with faint damnation, is epigrammatic: "We know that war is ugly, and that the *Iliad* is beautiful."[43] "Some nations have not lasted as long as Rome fell."[44] "History smiles at all attempts to force its flow into theoretical patterns or logical grooves; it plays havoc with our generalizations, breaks all our rules."[45] "It was a pity that Adrian could not understand the Renaissance; but it was a greater crime and folly that the Renaissance could not tolerate a Christian Pope."[46] "Like most martyrs, [Galileo] suffered for the right to be wrong."[47] "The state in some measure had civilized man, but who would civilize the state?"[48] "No nation is ever defeated in its textbooks."[49] Readers remember the Durants because readers remember their words—not all five million of them, but a pithy line here or there that somehow manages to put whole epochs into perspective.

The Story of Civilization flouted other historical conventions. The agnostic's pen ironically transformed the "dark ages" into the "age of faith." What is "dark" about an age that abolished gladiatorial contests, produced *The Divine Comedy,* invented eyeglasses, and constructed the Chartres Cathedral? Durant surmised, "We shall never do justice to the Middle Ages until we see the Italian Renaissance not as their repudiation but as their fulfillment."[50]

War attracts readers to history. In *The Story of Civilization,* in the most subtle manner, readers of history are gradually repulsed by war. We learn in *Our Oriental Heritage* that in 1197 crusading Mohammedans razed the magnificent Nalanda, the most prestigious Buddhist monastery in India.[51] In *The Life of Greece,* the reader is disgusted to discover that the Parthenon became ruins after Venetians fired upon it in 1687 when Turks had used it as a munitions storehouse, and that the Acropolis was the most famous casualty of the Greek War of Independence of the 1820s.[52] *The Age of Reason Begins* reports that in Munich alone, World War II claimed the Bavarian royalty's Residenz, the Antiquarium museum of ancient statues, and the huge Renaissance church St. Michael's.[53] The reader of history is often strangely obtuse to war's anonymous human costs. These lost historical treasures hit the antiquarian where it hurts.

The Durants managed to attract millions of readers to *The Story of Civilization* despite the fact that the eleven-volume behemoth approaches ten thousand pages and says almost nothing about the time and place inhabited by its readers. *The Story of Civilization* was multicultural before multicultural was cool. From the first volume in the series—a 1,047-page tome focusing exclusively on Islam, India, the Orient, and other exotica—readers learn that Westerners took the practice of writing left to right from the Babylonians; that the Chinese bequeathed a seismograph, paper money, and a compass more than a millennium before Christ; and that the Hindus gave Europeans "Arabic" numerals.[54] If being confronted with the vast contributions of the long dead and far away doesn't shake readers out of their provincialism, then the Durants' occasional exposure of the provincialism of foreigners does. *The Story of Civilization* spotlights the Japanese Shogun Iyeyasu's decree exiling Christians from the island nation and points out that Ibn Khaldun's three-volume *Muqaddama al-Almat*—literally, an introduction to the universe—devotes a scant seven pages to Christianity.[55] Parochialism is the most cosmopolitan of faults.

The Durants—or Will at least—also rejected the historian's intrusion into history. "If I were to ask what Will Durant believes, or disbelieves," a correspondent lamented, "I could not produce a single paragraph *explicitly* stating your position." What some readers, and even his wife, viewed as criticism, Will considered compliment.[56] Though the pair's politics was largely a closed book in their books, Citizen Will and Citizen Ariel were far from shrinking violets.

In 1930, Durant spent a weekend with Herbert Hoover at Camp Rapidan, where the philosopher conversed with the president for hours and bested Charles Lindbergh, whom he had earlier bested on 1927's best-seller list, in ping-pong. By 1932, Durant shifted his allegiance to Franklin Roosevelt, who hosted him at the White House in 1936, as did his successor, Harry Truman, who assured Durant that he kept a volume of *The Story of Civilization* by his bed for evening reading. The couple's passion for Hubert Humphrey so clouded judgment that, in the last days of the 1968 campaign, they mixed the name of his California Quaker adversary with Nazis and the Ku Klux Klan.[57] Seeing the past did not translate into telling the future. Will voted for Woodrow Wilson to stay out of the Great War, Franklin Roosevelt to stay out of World War II, and Lyndon Johnson to stay out of Vietnam.[58] To his credit, he highlighted, rather than obscured, his mistakes, such as his belief that Imperial Japan would never attack America and his early enthusiasm for anarchist education, "a weak inability on our own part to command because we had never learned to obey."[59] His fondness for the solutions of political medicine men extended to quack remedies. An enema bag stood out as a strange travel companion and his plate generally allowed no room for flesh.[60]

But by the 1960s, the onetime social and educational director of Camp Utopia sounded like a reactionary.[61] "Most of our literature and social philosophy, after 1850, was the voice of freedom against authority, of the child against the parent, of the pupil against the teacher, of men against the state," Durant reflected in 1963. "I shared in that individualistic revolt. I do not regret that rebellion; it is the function of youth to defend liberty and innovation, of the old to defend order and tradition, and of middle age to find a middle way. But now that I too am old, I wonder whether the battle I fought was not too completely won. Have we too much freedom? Have we so long ridiculed authority in the family, discipline in education, rules in art, decency in conduct, and law in the State that our liberation has brought us close to chaos in the family and the school, in morals, arts, ideas, and Government? We forgot to make ourselves intelligent when we made ourselves free."[62]

If ever a man embodied the Churchillism that conservatism in youth reveals heartlessness and liberalism in age reveals brainlessness, Will Durant did. Three decades after his reality check on Soviet Communism, Durant again became a man against fashion with his broadside against the ascendant moral anarchism. In politics, religion, marriage, and scholarship, Durant forever played the apostate.

The End of *Civilization*

One constant through the decades was work. The dropout seminarian of Seton Hall morphed into the monk of the Hollywood Hills. Only occasionally would he emerge from his hermitage to take in a movie, catch a concert at the Hollywood Bowl, or party with the likes of Charlie Chaplin, Bob Hope, and Douglas Fairbanks. On the typical day, Durant emigrated from his bed to his desk's rocking chair, where he worked—save for meals, walks, and swims—from 8 A.M. to 10 P.M. He aimed for one thousand words a day, a pace that allowed for a *Story of Civilization* entry every four years or so. The disciplined schedule generally held for more than four decades.[63] As Ariel matter-of-factly pointed out, "How else would we get it done?"[64]

While each new volume soared onto the best-seller lists, the critics regularly stung the Durants. On the eve of the publication date for *The Story of Civilization*'s eighth volume, Simon and Schuster's double-page *New York Times Book Review* advertisement called *The Age of Louis XIV* a "work of wisdom, winged with wit."[65] The issue's commissioned review painted a different picture: "facile," "shoddy," and "unworthy," sneered J. H. Plumb, a Cambridge University historian. Plumb pulled no punches in the 1963 critique: "Firstly, the Durants' scholarship is deplorable." If the contest between historians were a prize fight, mercy would have compelled an immediate stoppage. Within a single section on the ascension of William and Mary, Professor Plumb exposed numerous errors. Mistakes, he wrote, "stud the book like stars in the heavens on a frosty night, but there are worse faults than errors of fact." Here, Plumb's mudslinging dirtied himself more than his adversaries. The "worse faults than errors of fact," according to Plumb, included ignoring contemporary historians.[66] Hell hath no fury like a professor left out of a bibliography. Nevertheless, in terms of venue, substance, and the critic's authority, Plumb's serves as the epitome of a devastating review.

Missing among Plumb's myriad criticisms was the glaring fault of *The Story of Civilization*'s later volumes: the master generalists had become second-rate specialists. The Durants had run out of history—the world's and their own. They wrote more about less.

In 1935, upon the release of *The Story of Civilization*'s inaugural volume, the *New York Times* announced four future volumes of what it called "a titanic undertaking."[67] By 1944's release of *Caesar and Christ,* the plan was still to finish *The Story of Civilization* in five volumes.[68] "If Mr. Durant's health and eyesight permit," Orville Prescott of the *New York Times* explained upon *The Age of Faith*'s 1950 release, "there will be a fifth volume in 1955 on the Renaissance and Reformation and a sixth in 1960 on the Age of Reason."[69] But the volume on the Renaissance and the Reformation split into separate books, so as five became six, six became seven. Upon the 1961 release of *The Age of Reason Begins, Time* magazine informed: "What was planned as Durant's final volume is now become part of a trilogy—with *The Age of Louis XIV* (1963) and *The Age of Voltaire* (1965) still ahead."[70] In 1967 *Time* reported, "*Rousseau and Revolution,* the tenth volume of the Durants' Story of Civilization, is the last."[71] But the couple returned for yet another curtain call in 1975 with *The Age of Napoleon,* and even entertained the idea of a twelfth volume, *The Age of Darwin.*[72]

Whereas *The Age of Faith*—the best book Ariel had ever read; the best book Will had ever written—covered the history of Jews, Christians, and Muslims over a millennium, the planned *Age of Reason* coda (the volumes that credit Ariel as coauthor) expanded to five books covering a mere 250 years and too often limiting focus to Britain and France. Whether betraying an Enlightenment bias, a concession to specialist historians, a Durants Inc. mania for more and more product, or age's desire to continue youth's activity, the extension of five volumes into eleven resulted in a lengthy encore that left the audience wanting less rather than more.

But in life's twilight, with their bodies and books in decline, came appreciation from quarters that hadn't always appreciated. Universities coveted the independent scholars as commencement speakers. Young people were introduced to the senior-citizen scribes through endless printings of *The Story of Civilization* and *The Story of Philosophy*. Critics awarded the criticized the Pulitzer Prize for *Rousseau and Revolution* in 1968. A Republican president bestowed the Medal of Freedom upon the stalwart Democrats in 1977. By November 1981, just days after Ariel's burial, the Catholic Church that had excommunicated Will administered his last rites.

"As a young man, he asked too many questions to be an authentic rebel," former *Saturday Review* editor Norman Cousins eulogized, "and in his later years he was too distrustful of the answers to be an authentic conservative."[73] Will and Ariel Durant became what they had wished history to become: for Democrats and Republicans, old and young, believers and atheists, scholars and readers—for everyone.

2

The People's Professor

How a High School Dropout Launched
the Great Books Movement

"I remember being shocked by the applause that greeted Will Durant when he was introduced by his publishers to this august assemblage," Mortimer Adler reflected on *The Story of Philosophy* author's appearance at 1926's International Congress of Philosophy held at Harvard University. "I sat there wishing that I could rise and read aloud my review of his book, due to appear the following week."[1]

That review and Alder's reflection upon the episode spoke more about the insecure young man's envy of Durant's blockbuster than it did about the blockbuster itself. Commissioned by Adler's friend Mark Van Doren, the review was colored by jealousy. One needn't have put Adler on the couch to understand that he didn't object to Durant's project as much as to the fact that Durant rather than Adler had produced it. Adler complained that Durant's *Story of Philosophy* suffered from "a vaudevillian character," "superficial clarity," and a readability that contributed to its dangerousness. "*The Story of Philosophy* is a very good book of its kind," the passive-aggressive reviewer explained in *The Nation*. "But what of its kind? Plato was clear on this point. The poets were banished for writing stories about the gods. Diogenes and Mr. Durant would have been exiled with them for telling stories about the philosophers."[2]

The five-star "Generalist Adler" to friends, "the Lawrence Welk of the philosophy trade" to foes, Mortimer Adler ironically became synonymous with popularizing high ideas to middlebrow minds.[3] "What puzzles me, as I look back at it now, is why I was so vehemently opposed to the popularization of knowledge at a time when I was so vigorously engaged in popularizing the great books and the great ideas," Adler observed in his first autobiography, *Philosopher at Large*. "The only explanation I can give is that I must have felt, somewhat smugly, that our kind of popularization (the kind that Everett Dean Martin, Scott Buchanan, Richard McKeon, and I were promoting at the People's Institute) was sound and beneficial, while their kind (the kind represented by the current best sellers, such as Durant's Story of Philosophy), was misguided and injurious."[4] A turf war between two similar outfits—the Labor Temple and the People's Institute—and envy at the success of a graduate of the same Columbia philosophy department that had exiled Adler to psychology to pursue his Ph.D., rather than any substantive differences, do much to explain the tiff.

Fourteen years after writing the papal bull excommunicating Durant from the scholarly ranks for writing for a mass audience, Adler cemented his own pariah status by penning *How to Read a Book*, the second best-selling nonfiction book of 1940.[5] "The original sin of

Adler's academic career was that he wrote a best-seller, *How to Read a Book*," Notre Dame's Ralph McInerny opined.[6] An intelligent lay audience, not scholarly peers, devoured Adler's annual and even semiannual offerings. In the thirty-five years starting with 1958 and ending in 1992, for instance, Adler cranked out more than thirty books—the public intellectual equivalent of the rock star stuffing a sock in his trousers.

Compounding Adler's difficulties among traditional intellectuals was his supersized ego, which did not go over well in a world of supersized egos.

Studying at Columbia, Adler amused himself by badgering the famous philosopher John Dewey with weekly letters pointing out the inconsistencies in his lectures. The teacher initially tolerated his student's critiques, but eventually tired of the lengthy missives and instructed an assistant to convey his displeasure.[7] Adler never let up on Dewey for the next seven decades. As *l'enfant terrible* of the University of Chicago, the brash twentysomething arrived in the philosophy department in Hyde Park and sparked resignations, recriminations, and ultimately his own exile to the school of law.[8] Gertrude Stein found Adler so insufferable at a dinner party that she bonked him atop the head, lecturing: "I am not going to argue any further with you, young man. I can see that you are the kind of young man who is accustomed to winning arguments."[9] When his Encyclopedia Britannica boss, William Benton, a former Madison Avenue ad tycoon, diplomat, and senator, wrote to Adler that he did not understand one of his points, the mischievous narcissist penned in the margins, "He's right; he doesn't."[10] To Henry Simon of Simon and Schuster, who had the temerity to offer revisions to a manuscript,

Adler wished for "the opportunity to conduct a private seminar for you on the subject." The publisher's "mistakes," the author noted, "should be corrected; and I am the man to do it." Adler offered to play Socrates to Simon's Glaucon.[11]

Teachers, colleagues, betters, bosses, and editors would find Mortimer Adler a difficult man.

But the difficult task of transforming Americans into the most educated people in history would require a difficult man. Who else but an egomaniac would devote his life to the ambitious—nay, utopian—proposition of making the education fit for a king the education for everyone?

The St. Paul of the Great Books

Charles Eliot's "Harvard Classics" sparked Adler's interest in the Great Books. Spotting Eliot's "five-foot shelf," Adler got a glimpse of Plato. Eliot's abridged texts served as a gateway drug to the unabridged Athenian. Adler, who had quit high school to become a copy boy at the *New York Sun*, quickly reassessed his calling from journalism to philosophy.[12]

That Charles Eliot jump-started Adler's interest in the classics proved one of the strange paradoxes of the life of the philosopher at large. For the Harvard University president became the bogeyman of the Great Books movement. "Mr. Eliot, more than any other man," Samuel Eliot Morison wrote in *Three Centuries of Harvard*, "is responsible for the greatest educational crime of the century against American youth—depriving him of his classical heritage."[13] The longest-serving president in Harvard's history, Eliot spearheaded the specialized "elective" curriculum that replaced the core curriculum, which had provided a common ground to the liberally educated. Many schools followed Harvard's lead.

"After leaving Harvard, Eliot profited from the changes he instituted while its president," Tim Lacy writes in a doctoral dissertation on the Great Books. "By allowing the diminishment of the classics' importance at Harvard, and setting a far-reaching precedent through his promotion of the elective system, he *almost* necessitated the various correctives that would follow. The Harvard Classics, and later the Great Books, helped fill this void. Eliot probably did not desire this chain of events, but he nevertheless was central in decreasing the prominence of the classics in higher education."[14] In debasing the Great Books within the academy, and by promoting them for profit outside of it, Charles Eliot helped create both the void Adler would fill and the model that Adler would follow. Eliot also created one of his own fiercest critics.

Born to Jewish immigrant parents on December 28, 1902, Mortimer Jerome Adler grew up in Manhattan. Double-promoted three times in the New York City public schools, Adler absorbed a sense of academic entitlement at a young age. If he could make the cash-strapped schools of Gotham acknowledge his brilliance by allowing him to skip grades, why need he bother with the perfunctory academic requirements of high school and college? Just give him the paper and get it over with. This mentality resulted in Adler's earning "the rare distinction . . . of being possibly the only Ph.D. in the country without a master's degree, bachelor's degree, or even a high school diploma."[15] But even this understates his contempt for academic norms. Adler played truant to the courses supposedly essential to attaining his doctorate. Earning a healthy income teaching classes at Columbia, City College, and the People's Institute, the graduate student found schoolwork a nuisance to his intellectual interests and financial ambitions. He outsourced the research for his psychology dissertation to struggling students at a dollar an hour. When his fleet of stringers completed the research, Adler cranked out a seventy-seven page dissertation in one twenty-hour session.[16]

Had it not been for a single class, Adler might have found coursework at Columbia largely a waste. He had been given an unearned doctorate and made important friends. But the life of the mind that breathed outside of Morningside Heights classrooms suffocated within. John Erskine's General Honors course stood as the exception. For two school years, students read an assigned classic every week. Rather than provide answers, the professor asked questions. Here, Adler found a religion in the Great Books. Here, Erskine found a St. Paul to spread the gospel according to Aristotle, Aquinas, Shakespeare, and Locke.

Erskine's reintroduction of the classics, in a mere course rather than in the entire curriculum, was very much a reaction against the zeitgeist created by Charles Eliot and John Dewey, whose educational theories denigrating books as constricting tools and a core of classes as an affront to student autonomy appalled the Great Bookies. Columbia took several years to approve his course, and Erskine launched it only after returning home from successfully administering a temporary university for idling soldiers at Beaune, France, at the close of the First World War.[17] The experience overseeing the soldier-scholars instilled confidence in Erskine that ordinary minds contained extraordinary capabilities. It colored the egalitarian philosophy behind encouraging unexceptional people to read exceptional books. Erskine opined that "the men who wrote these books, would have been horrified if they had known that you and I might think of them only as matter for school and college courses. They wrote to be read by the general public, and they assumed in their readers an experience of life and an interest in human nature, nothing more."[18]

The egalitarian mission of spreading the wisdom of elite minds to the masses, then, characterized the Great Books movement from the beginning. Adler picked up Erskine's torch and ran with it in his own direction. He first taught the Great Books at Columbia, and then, along with Whittaker Chambers, Jacques Barzun, Clifton Fadiman, Richard McKeon, and Mark Van Doren, at the People's Institute to adults interested in continuing education. For twenty-five cents, daylight workers *cum* night-school students—anywhere from a few dozen to more than a hundred—imbibed hour-long lectures followed by an hour's discussion.[19] Adler transitioned from teaching at this sans-accreditation "people's university," which begged students for quarters, to teaching at one of the world's most prestigious universities, founded by the world's wealthiest inhabitant.[20]

"Why Don't We Do That?"

Upstart professor Mortimer Adler had early on caught the ear of upstart university administrator Robert Maynard

Hutchins. At first glance, the towering preacher's son and the gnomish firstborn of a Manhattan jeweler made quite a contrast. Beneath the surface, their commonalities eluded puzzled observers. Both were scholarship students: Hutchins washed dishes and worked in a factory to put himself through Yale; Adler brown-bagged it and saved subway fare by trudging twenty-five blocks to attend Columbia.[21] First in his class at Yale Law, the second-generation college administrator took the fast track to the academic aristocracy by stepping in as dean of his prestigious law school alma mater at twenty-eight. Two years later, in 1929, Hutchins became president of the University of Chicago at just thirty years old. The magnetic new university president wanted his friend's advice.

"Now, I know nothing about education," Hutchins confessed to Adler upon his selection to lead Chicago. "I am now president of one of the great universities of the country—in fact, one of the two greatest universities of the country—and I have to begin thinking about education. Have you any ideas?"

"I've never thought about education, either," Adler responded. "But I do know something about my own education. The only education I got at Columbia was in one course."

Chicago's fifth president asked, "What was that?"

"The Great Books course," explained Erskine's former student. "The rest of it I will forget. The only thing that's going to affect my life, so far as I can see, are the books I read and the discussions I had in that one course."

Hutchins responded, "Well, why don't we do that?"[22]

And so they did. Or at least they tried.

Though the University of Chicago would long be associated with the Great Books, institutional inertia prevented Hutchins from remaking the school in the image that he and Adler had in mind. Hutchins succeeded in slaying the "Monsters of the Midway," the school's football program, which he saw as a non sequitur for an academic institution. But his success in transforming the curriculum was limited. He laid out his lost cause in the 1936 book *The Higher Learning in America*. Therein, he called for the abolition of departments to unify the disparate parts of the modern university; the exile of professional training to the professions themselves or to technical schools; a common general education focusing on Great Books; and a curriculum designed by educators rather than electives chosen by the uneducated. Education for its own sake, rather than education driven by a utilitarian or financial purpose, was his overriding aim.[23] Rather than despise their hard-to-despise Adonis-like president, professors resistant to change directed their ire at his troll-like sidekick. Adler was an academic punching bag, albeit one who hit back—*hard*.

Though Hutchins and Adler failed to transform the University of Chicago into a Great Books school, they succeeded, here and there, in promoting the classics. Specifically, they targeted incoming freshmen by offering a course modeled on Erskine's Great Books class. They also started a continuing education Great Books program. Targeted at local businessmen, it was nicknamed the Fat Man's Class.

One of the prized students in the Fat Man's Class was William Benton, who, along with his wife, enrolled in the fall of 1943. In the 1930s, Benton had made a killing as half of the powerhouse Benton & Bowles advertising agency. Since amassing his fortune, he had split his time between entrepreneurialism and service, with the former including the acquisition of Encyclopedia Britannica in 1943 and the latter including the acceptance of a vice presidency under Hutchins at the University of Chicago. Benton's worlds of capitalism and altruism collided in the Great Books. "Benton . . . in preparing himself for the discussions, found that it was not easy to get his hands on the great books," notes biographer Sydney Hyman. "Many, to be sure, were available through one publisher or another—if one had time to ferret them out. Many were also available in a library—if one had time to go to a library, and if someone else was not reading the single copy on hand. To Benton, all this seemed to be a conspiracy against his time. To put a stop to the evil, he proposed to Hutchins and Adler that the Britannica company had an obligation—and an opportunity—to publish a set of the great books."[24]

The idea moved neither Hutchins nor Adler until the subject of differentiating the Encyclopedia Britannica set from Eliot's Harvard Classics through an index was broached.[25] Reading an entire set of hundreds of books put too high an expectation on the average reader. But providing an index for what the Great Books say about the great ideas would make the set more accessible, efficient, relevant, and useful. As had been done with "encyclopedia" and "dictionary," Adler invented a word, "syntopicon"—meaning a synthesis of topics—to name the learning aid. The subsequent ad copy explained that "the amazing Syntopicon makes the wisdom of the Great Books available *instantly* to anyone." In other words, one needn't read all the way through to benefit from the Great Books. "The Syntopicon makes owning and using the Great Books far more practical than ever before," Encyclopedia Britannica boasted. "It's like having a great teacher living in your home with you, always available at your beck and call."[26]

"The First Intellectual Assembly Line in History"

But what books would Alder index?

As Adler recruited his indexing staff, Hutchins put together a board to decide which books merited the designation "great." The close-knit group was built for conformity rather than for conflict. After all, the enthusiasts of the classics, in contrast to the critics, had read a sufficient number to differentiate the greats from the not-so-greats. The University of Chicago chieftain chaired in theory, but his frequent absences made Adler chairman in practice.[27] John Erskine and his apostles peopled a majority of the board. Joining Adler again was Mark Van Doren, who, since team-teaching a Great Books course at Columbia with the Great Bookie himself, had gained fame as a poet. Scott Buchanan, who had facilitated Adler's Great Books course at the People's Institute and subsequently transformed the ancient St. John's College into a Great Books institution, joined the board. In turn, Buchanan's mentor, Alexander Meiklejohn, former president and philosophy professor at Amherst College (where Erskine had once taught), and Stringfellow Barr, a Rhodes Scholar alongside Buchanan at Oxford and a partner in the rejuvenation of St. John's, came aboard, too. Hutchins also added allies at the University of Chicago: Dean Clarence Faust and chemistry professor Joseph Schwab.

As foreshadowed by the composition of the board, the books chosen leaned heavily toward philosophy.

Overriding Adler's initial objections and Erskine's sentiment that science belongs in a laboratory and not in book discussion groups, the set embraced the St. John's College approach of including pioneering works of math and science that, however foundational for modern mathematicians and scientists, glaze over the eyes of contemporary readers, even ones versed in such fields.[28] As book critic Clifton Fadiman later cynically said of the obscure mathematics volumes, "people want these *names* on their shelves; therefore, from the sales and promotion viewpoints *only*, they should be included."[29] Apollonius, Nicomachus, and Ptolemy remained.

Generally, the closer a book was to the present, the more intense the debate on the committee.[30] "Molière will go out only over my bruised body," Mark Van Doren announced.[31] But go he did, as did Dickens, Calvin, and Voltaire. Though a 1990 revision of the Great Books included such authors, the passage of time has mostly vindicated the committee rather than its critics. The proximity of a book to our rearview mirror tends to distort its greatness. The committee did fall prey to some intellectual fads. When, for instance, but during the on-the-couch postwar years, would Freud have been awarded an entire volume?

Dwight Macdonald, one of the first and most trenchant critics of *The Great Books of the Western World*, observed a "fetish for Great Writers" rather than Great Books. "Minor works by major writers are consistently preferred to major works by minor writers. Thus nearly all Shakespeare is here, including even 'The Two Gentlemen of Verona,' but not Marlowe's 'Dr. Faustus' or Webster's 'Duchess of Malfi' or Jonson's 'Volpone.' Nearly all Milton's poetry is here, but no Donne, no Herrick, no

Marvell, or, for that matter, any other English poetry except Chaucer and Shakespeare. We get Gibbon in two huge volumes but no Vico, Michelet, or Burckhardt; six hundred pages of Kant but no Nietzsche or Kierkegaard; two volumes of Aquinas but no Calvin or Luther; three hundred pages of Montesquieu's 'Spirit of Laws,' but no Voltaire or Diderot."[32] It was a subjective list that omitted many great books and included a few not-so-great ones.

More laborious, and expensive, than the selection of the Great Books was the selection, and indexing, of the great ideas therein. Adler and his team of 4-Fs, grad students, and bookworms mined the Great Books for the great ideas they contained. They came up with 102 (e.g., infinity, duty, sin, truth). Then came the hard part: finding passages relevant to each of the 102 great ideas within the 443 works included in the Great Books, plus the Bible (which was considered a "Great Book" but not included in the set because of its widespread availability and the danger of offending consumers by embracing a particular version). Indexing, a tedious endeavor for one book, became exponentially more laborious given the enormous scope of works covered and the particular indexing involved here: thematic indexing, which poses more difficulties than indexing, say, people or places. One hundred twenty-five people worked on the Syntopicon at its peak, with the Chicago workers converging on Index House, a gray building on the University of Chicago campus that served as "the first intellectual assembly line in history."[33] What was intended to cost $60,000 and take two years cost almost $1 million and took seven years.

Allowing Mortimer Adler to spend someone else's money was a bad idea. As Adler remembered it, "Bill

Benton never forgot, and never quite forgave, the enormous discrepancy between the original estimate and the final cost."[34] The Syntopicon nearly derailed not only *The Great Books of the Western World* but Encyclopedia Britannica as well. Benton personally loaned Britannica $350,000, purchased its collection of paintings for $82,000, convinced the University of Chicago to assume a $1 million debenture, canceled bonuses, and tasked salesmen with sales *and* collections.[35] The Syntopicon project underwent a "radical revision" in late 1947 that delayed into the 1950s the publication date of *The Great Books of the Western World*. As an Encyclopedia Britannica memo explained, "The work which would have been done under the previous plan by over 20 persons will now, under the present plan, have to be done by three."[36]

Encyclopedia Britannica was all in. Benton and company were committed to seeing *The Great Books of the Western World*, and its accompanying money-pit index, through.

A Frenetic Pace

Rather than relieving Adler of his responsibilities for pushing the project over budget, Benton decided that Mortimer made the mess, so Mortimer should clean it up. Begging Adler to "please lay off of me all you can," soon-to-be senator Benton reiterated in 1949 that "we want you to take all responsibility and leadership on all aspects of the problems involved in the Great Books."[37] If Encyclopedia Britannica's project were a hockey team, Mortimer Adler would have played center, defenseman, goalie, and left and right wing. Between periods he would have piloted the Zamboni and sharpened skates. In every part of the publishing process, there was Adler.

With the project imperiled, Adler switched hats from philosopher to salesman, a line of work his critics long believed the entrepreneurial academic better suited for. "In desperation, I went to Bill Benton and Harry Houghton with a plan for raising $250,000 to defray the cost of printing and binding 2,500 sets," Adler recalled. "It involved selling a numbered edition of 500 sets at $500 a set to individuals who would be listed as patrons of the enterprise."[38] He reasoned that "many of the great books could not have been written without Patrons; it is not surprising that they cannot now be republished without Patrons. The top men in our society can be asked to join the company of Alexander the Great, Augustus Caesar, Maecenas, the Earl of Essex, the Earl of Shaftsbury, King James, etc., as Patrons of the Great Books."[39] Again, the Great Books mixed the worlds of entrepreneurialism and philanthropy.

Adler drafted a letter that went out under Hutchins's signature to a thousand fat cats soliciting $500 for the privilege of receiving a special "Founders Edition" set of *The Great Books of the Western World*. The direct-mail solicitation generated a remarkable 25 percent return rate. The pair transitioned to the personal ask. Hutchins and Adler managed to hector hotel magnate Conrad Hilton, CBS chief executive William Paley, banking heir Paul Mellon, Harold Linder of General American Investors, filmmaker Frank Capra, and *Washington Post* publisher Eugene Meyer into purchasing the "special buckram binding" edition at $500 a set.[40]

Adler acted as the original door-to-door salesman of the Great Books, knocking on the gates of the rich

and powerful. By April 1, 1951, Britannica had 419 sub-
scriptions; by October, 453. With payment still forth-
coming from many subscribers, and the campaign to
add patrons ongoing, Britannica had already collected
$185,000—$20,000 short of breaking even on the production of the 500 bound volumes and another 2,000
warehoused, unbound, unsold sets.[41] On April 15, 1952,
Britannica delivered its buckram-bound Founders Edition to subscribers at a gala dinner. Held in New York's
Waldorf-Astoria, and attended by the likes of Conrad
Hilton, Nelson Rockefeller, and Alfred Vanderbilt, the
event, a media magnet by design, served as the promotional launch of the Great Books.

In anticipation of the set's release, Adler laid out an
ambitious promotional strategy. He acted as architect
and bricklayer. He made a personal visit to Columbia
classmate Henry Morton Robinson of *Reader's Digest*,
dialed up old friend Clifton Fadiman to pen an essay
on the set in *Holiday* and commission a review for the
New Yorker, and appeared on NBC Radio's *University of
Chicago Round Table* to gin up interest in the set.[42] When
Adler informed interviewer Clare Booth Luce that initially only a thousand sets would be made available,
Luce played the role of booster to perfection: "I should
not think that that would be enough. I think that every
single library, every college, in the whole country must
have this first and entirely new reference book."[43] Adler
pitched *The Great Books of the Western World* to eighteen
editors during a three-day trip to New York at the end
of October 1951. The marathon of presentations ranged
from thirty minutes to six hours.[44] The masterfully
orchestrated campaign culminated with a *Time* cover
story on Adler coinciding with the release of the set.[45]

Planning and persistence tell part of the story of the media frenzy propelling the Great Books. The trio behind the Britannica set was among America's best connected men. Benton gained entry into the U.S. Senate through an appointment by his former business partner, Chester Bowles, the governor of Connecticut. Hutchins's frequent appearances in *Time* owed much to the fact that his Yale classmate Henry Luce owned the media giant. Adler could count on the praises of America's foremost middlebrow literary critic, Fadiman, who was one of his closest friends. These were networkers extraordinaire whose tentacles extended into business, politics, Hollywood, media, and academia.

In addition to targeting cultural middlemen, the trio took the marketing campaign directly to the public. The ad copy aimed at the masses was derived in large part from Adler's statistic-laden Encyclopedia Britannica memorandums.[46] The set contained "443 works by 74 great authors from Homer to Freud!" Therein were "24,000,000 words" printed on "32,000 pages" in "54 distinctive volumes." The project involved "400,000 man-hours of selection," with the Syntopicon requiring "163,000 exact references after making 900,000 reference decisions."[47] In the social-science-obsessed 1950s, numbers, even ones arrived at by guesswork, impressed.

Adler even managed to incorporate digs at Eliot into the ads. In a 1950 corporate memo to the former ad tycoon Benton, Adler pointed out that whereas the then unpublished Great Books contained 25,600,000 words, Eliot's Harvard Classics contained a mere 8,100,000; whereas the Harvard Classics excerpted more than half of their inclusions, the Great Books printed unabridged texts in 99 percent of cases; and whereas the "Great

Books vary in bulk and typographical design," the Harvard Classics "have the deadly appearance of a *set* of books." Even as petty an observation as the "paper of the Harvard Classics is of a quality inferior to the paper chosen for the Great Books" found its way into the exhaustive comparison.[48] Great Books v. Harvard Classics was Coke v. Pepsi, Ford v. GM, Microsoft v. Apple. Adler's memo made it into Britannica's negative advertising. "Do the Harvard Classics Meet Today's Demand for Great Books?" Britannica's promotional copy asked. "The Harvard Classics are extracts; the GREAT BOOKS are COMPLETE," answered one of the ad's comparative points cribbed from Adler's memo.[49] Not to be outdone by the Great Books' "Syntopicon," the Harvard Classics countered with the "Idexicon."[50] Evidence of their triumph, Adler later pointed out, was "the great books" replacing "the classics" in the popular vernacular.[51]

Adler gave pep talks to the sales force, appeared in urban department stores, starred in a promotional film, and even cut an ill-fated Great Books record intended to be used as a sales premium.[52] He identified the best translations.[53] He wrote a syndicated column on the Great Books. Even as nuts-and-bolts a publishing matter as ordering paper ensnared Adler: Truman administration controls on paper mills resulted in shortages, and securing the requisite amount of paper presented a considerable obstacle for a fifty-four-volume production.[54]

Adler's frenetic pace was nothing short of amazing. Making the publishing feat all the more remarkable was his numerous side activities during the years he helped produce *The Great Books of the Western World*. He secured a grant of $655,000 to found the Institute for Philosophical Research. He taught at the University of

Chicago, accepted outside lecture invitations at $350 an appearance, and acted as a highly paid consultant to the cinema's Hays Office.[55] He taught his Fat Man's Class in Chicago and added another at the Aspen Institute. In these years, he established the tradition of speaking at St. John's College, which provoked a tradition among listeners of playing practical jokes, such as a pizza deliveryman or a marble avalanche interrupting the lecture.[56] He traveled as an ambassador of the Great Books Foundation to the libraries of more than a dozen U.S. cities, with his lecture on how to establish discussion groups becoming the manual on the subject.[57] Other than the finished product itself, the only visible evidence that Mortimer Adler had engaged in a massive project in these years is the conspicuous decade-long gap between books on his curriculum vitae.[58] Who has time to write a book when one is republishing great ones?

Adler played as hard as he worked. *Time* magazine described him as "a martini-sipping scholastic iconoclast" who "likes Brooks Brothers suits, good leather, fast cars, fine food."[59] *Time* didn't mention that he also liked women. He proposed marriage to a girlfriend five months before proposing divorce to his wife, whom he manipulated into suing him for divorce.[60] He subsequently married a third woman, more than thirty years his junior. Reading Great Books didn't necessarily make one a good man.

Selling the Great Books

All of Adler's marketing missed the masses—at least initially. *The Great Books of the Western World* enticed 1,863 buyers in its first year; the next, just 138.[61] Listen to the crickets. A power struggle ensued within Encyclopedia Britannica between Robert Hutchins, the Great Books devotee who had recently departed the University of Chicago, and R. C. Preble, Britannica's new bottom-line-driven president.

"My recommendation . . . is that we spend a few thousand dollars to develop a couple of hundred sales outfits—as complete as we can make them," Preble wrote to Adler a year before publication. "About half of these outfits should be apportioned to our 15 Division Managers, from perhaps three for the Denver Office to a dozen or more for New York City. Additional sales outfits would then be provided where activity developed." Preble believed Encyclopedia Britannica could recoup $25,000 to $35,000 for every thousand sets sold through salesmen.[62] If the people wouldn't come to the Great Books, the Great Books would come to the people. And they did so in the gauche manner that the academic president Hutchins had initially feared.[63]

After war and depression let loose a frenzy of pent-up consumption, but before malls and door-to-door rapists killed the traveling salesman, the pedestrian pitchman enjoyed a golden age. Hoover vacuums, Oneida flatware, remedies of debatable effectiveness, and *The Great Books of the Western World* were among the products that salesmen unloaded upon neighborhoods across an increasingly suburban America. That the consumption explosion coincided with the midcentury craze of intellectual betterment—the GI Bill, the Book-of-the-Month Club, "university of the air"–style radio programs—made for a fortuitous collision between the mood of the market and Encyclopedia Britannica's marketing. People not only wanted to buy; they wanted to buy what Adler, Benton, and Hutchins were selling through their door-to-door evangelists.

Who bought?

"Let's go after the mass market—the butcher, the baker, the candlestick maker," explained super sales-man Kenneth Harden. By tapping Harden to move stagnant Great Books sets in 1956, Encyclopedia Britannica ensured that those who had proclaimed the venture "Benton's Folly" would have egg on their faces. But Harden's rhetoric of targeting the everyman was more sales pitch than objective reality. In contrast to, say, library-run Great Books discussion groups—priced right at free—sets of *The Great Books of the Western World* ranged from $298 to $1,175 (roughly $2,300 to $9,700 in 2011 dollars). The owners of the Great Books unsurprisingly worked as doctors, engineers, accountants, teachers, business owners, and other white-collar professionals. Laborers, farmers, craftsmen, and foremen conspicuously represented just 5 percent of buyers.[64] More than half the customers had graduated from college at a time when college degrees were extraordinary.[65] Middle- and upper-income earners predominated.[66] The blue-collar intellectuals who thrived in Great Books discussion groups were not the buyers of the commodity sold as the Great Books.

How did Americans come to purchase *The Great Books of the Western World*? Buyers first encountered the set through magazine advertising (35 percent), direct mail (17 percent), salesmen (14 percent), and friends/relatives (14 percent).[67] Almost a fifth bought the set never to read it at all.[68] "In general, owners actually use the Great Books infrequently," noted Marplan, the consumer research firm employed by Britannica to help it sell smarter, not harder. "The owners enjoy having the Great Books in the home and tend to use them when the occasion arises but not with regularity."[69] About half of all owners of the Great Books kept their sets in the living room.[70] "The owners relate to the Great Books as prized possessions to be displayed for others to see," Marplan theorized.[71] Whereas use tended to be the most common reason motivating the purchase of the set, just 7 percent of owners cited using the Great Books as what they liked about owning them.[72]

Whatever the buyers' motivation, Preble and Harden's door-to-door approach worked. In 1962, *Time* reported that the commission-driven field put as much as $30,000 annually into the pockets of Britannica salesmen and $100,000 into the pockets of its regional managers.[73] Adler, predictably, wanted a cut. "Their contribution to the sales effort is local," Adler reasoned of the traveling force, "and they get a percentage as long as they continue to make a contribution to sales. I would be making a contribution to the sales effort on a national basis! Why shouldn't I get a percentage of the sales on a national basis?"[74] The drive for commissions prompted inventive methods among the salesmen, including false representations of themselves as University of Chicago professors.[75] Ultimately, by means fair and foul, Encyclopedia Britannica sold more than one million sets. Though the University of Chicago had rebuffed William Benton's philanthropic attempt to deed Encyclopedia Britannica to it, the school banked more than $60 million from its involvement in Britannica's various capitalist enterprises.[76] Adler, later inaccurately describing his remunerated efforts as merely a "labor of love," nevertheless did not get the royalty he requested.[77]

Great Books in Mediocre Times

In the aftermath of World War II, and in the beginnings of the Cold War, Americans sought to discover what, precisely, they were fighting to preserve. The Great Books provided answers. They clued in readers to the building blocks upon which the West was built.

"Until lately the West has regarded it as self-evident that the road to education lay through great books," the introductory volume explained. "No man was educated unless he was acquainted with the masterpieces of his tradition."[78] This fundamental idea, like the West itself, was under attack—thus the rationale for *The Great Books of the Western World*. The set's editors explained that for the West to remain a community, the community must have something in common to communicate. The Great Books provided that. They also provided two other ingredients essential to a healthy republic: an educated citizenry and leisure that uplifted rather than debased. "If the people are not capable of acquiring this education, they should be deprived of political power and probably of leisure," the editors reasoned. "Their uneducated political power is dangerous, and their uneducated leisure is degrading and will be dangerous."[79] Americans in surprising numbers rose to the challenge issued by Adler, Hutchins, Benton, and their associates.

In 1948, *Parade* magazine introduced America to Winchester, Indiana, where the drugstore, railroad depot, and barbershop hosted impromptu debates over Chaucer, Aquinas, and the Declaration of Independence. Boosted by an anonymous offer of free books for anyone participating in reading groups of the classics, Winchester was one of two hundred communities then caught up in a renaissance of continuing education. Small-town Hoosierville—nurses, preachers, housewives, factory workers, retirees—met weekly in the high school gym to discuss the works of Plato, Plutarch, Augustine, Adam Smith, and other authors who transcended their place and time to reach mid-twentieth-century Middle America. Americana-meets-the-Academy was the result of the Hutchins-chaired Great Books Foundation, which Johnny-Appleseeded reading groups, trained volunteer discussion leaders, and printed cheap editions of the classics. "As democratic and gregarious as a husking bee, with no academic background requirements, no teachers, no tuition, no axes to grind, and no fees beyond the optional one of buying the Foundation's cheap, paper-bound editions of the texts, Great Books is probably the broadest cultural experiment ever attempted, a fact that has urged its adoption by labor unions, churches, women's clubs, Y's, factories, and, as in Winchester, cross sections of entire communities," the Sunday circular reported.[80]

Though the postwar years served as the heyday of the Great Books, it would be a mistake to consign the movement to Hula-Hoops, crowding into phone booths, and other midcentury fads. Adler taught his last Fat Man's Class in 1988, and Encyclopedia Britannica sent traveling salesmen home for good in 1997, but the Great Books endure.[81]

A teenaged Thomas Hyland hitchhiked from Colorado to Columbia, where he came upon the classics almost two decades after Adler had done so. He dropped out of school, but never dropped out of his education. He transitioned from flying bombers during World

War II to flying passengers for United, which afforded him much hurry-up-and-wait time to pursue his love of reading. Hyland's son remembers his passions as "reading Great Books and killing Japs." So overwhelming was the former passion that Hyland was buried with Adler's *How to Read a Book* and left sixty-three thousand other books for the living at his estate sale.[82]

David Call came upon Mortimer Adler one Sunday afternoon while watching public television during the early 1980s. He devoured Adler's books and quickly set about converting his fellow workers at Utah construction sites. They read books in their spare time and discussed them during lunch breaks. Countering the "John Deere" and "Michelob" hats popular among the laborers, Call's group took to wearing "Great Ideas" headwear. Overhearing the lunchtime philosophical dialogues, a bricklayer asked, "What is your philosophy on getting a good orgasm?" Even this taunt sparked a discussion. Call and his brother, also a plumber, enrolled in a philosophy course at the University of Utah and scored As.[83]

Jim Hellwig didn't much read or even vote before coming across the Great Books. He focused on bodybuilding, and then professional wrestling. After conquering the latter field by pinning Hulk Hogan at WrestleMania VI, the Ultimate Warrior, Hellwig's *nom de wrestler*, pursued a sound mind to complement his sound physique. Adler's *How to Read a Book* led Warrior to Aristophanes, Euripides, Plato, Homer, Aurelius, Plutarch, and the Great Books. "I can't read Homer or the classical philosophers without saying, 'Fuck, leave me the fuck alone!'" As the road consumed peers through overdoses and suicides, Warrior stuffed his gear bag with Great Books. "The very reason these guys aren't around today—and they behaved the way they did—is because they didn't have a philosophical perspective on life," Warrior explains of his many deceased wrestling colleagues. "They didn't make a connection between actions creating consequences." The Great Books helped Warrior sustain discipline. "Another great thing about getting into the Great Books is coming to the realization that philosophy is not some nebulous concept that only scholars and academics know something about." To this day, the Ultimate Warrior buys sets of *The Great Books of the Western World* as gifts for friends and family.[84]

That the Great Books movement outlived its founders is hardly surprising. If Aristotle's works could survive in a basement in Asia Minor, and Galileo could reach the present after numerous past bans, then the Great Books could weather the onslaught of TMZ.com, *Call of Duty*, and techno. There is always a market for great, especially when the base and the mediocre encroach.

The Riddle of the American Republic

From establishing world government to saving the ozone layer to compulsory service to the state, Mortimer Adler endorsed many political fads during his ninety-eight years.[85] But *the* cause of his century couldn't be more grating to the faddish cognoscenti. No number of oblations to the gods of fashion could undo that cardinal sin.

The Great Books movement sought to break learning from its confinement inside of formal schools. *Time* recognized the threat it posed the educational establishment when, beneath Mortimer Adler's visage, it provocatively asked, "Should professors commit suicide?"

on a 1952 cover.[86] The discussion groups that popped up in libraries and other community centers featured leaders who facilitated conversations, not teachers who instructed or passed judgment. When the Great Bookies got hold of a school, as they did at St. John's, professors became mere "tutors" and, like their understudies, were tasked with becoming liberally educated rather than specializing in fields of their choosing. Save for the "great ideas" essays and the Syntopicon, *The Great Books of the Western World* is essentially free of intermediaries. Far from a solitary endeavor, education for the Great Bookies was a group process, but one that need not involve formal schools. "*Education is the business of adults*," Adler stressed. "It is a major vocation of men and women, not a minor avocation. Adult education is *not* a hobby or pastime, a fifth wheel on the cart of education, when it is considered as it should be—as the occupation, not of childhood, but of a whole life."[87] This left traditional schools as one aspect, rather than the sum total, of education. The Great Books movement, for better and worse, offered education minus the middleman. It is no wonder the middleman objected so vociferously.

Initially, snobs sniffed that Adler and company had peddled the Great Books through Madison Avenue–style adverts, door-to-door salesmen, and department-store demonstrations. It was as though anything touched by the grubby hand of the merchant was thereby stained. "Culture," Dwight Macdonald lamented, "like any other commodity, must now be 'sold' to Americans."[88] Time has not been kind to this criticism. From today's perspective, the feat of generating so much interest in Aristotle and Aquinas, Homer and Hume, and Copernicus and Kant that people would be willing spend hundreds of dollars to obtain their writings seems praiseworthy, if a bit surreal. People spend money on scratch tickets, ringtones, and tanning. But Thucydides, Chaucer, and Cervantes?

The criticism shifted over time. "Hey, hey, ho, ho/ Western culture's got to go," famously chanted Stanford University protestors upset with required courses on the Western canon. For the campus-centered multiculturalists, the chief affront of the classics is that they are of the Western world. Those aiming to tear down Western civilization have little time to study its foundations. People who would never be so stupid to ask, "Where are the Swedish contributions to the great books of the Orient?" complain about the pale complexion of the authors behind *The Great Books of the Western World*. Who would have thought that Western civilization's best science, literature, history, and philosophy would have primarily been the work of Europeans? This demographically illiterate sentiment condemns the very notion of the Western tradition because that tradition inherently excludes Indians, Mongolians, and Ethiopians. It's too white, too male, and intolerant of the academic tic that demands syllabi boast authors of various hues (even if of the same outlook).

Just as some castigate the Great Books for being too white and too male, others think them too dead. The paucity of modern books seems a slur against the present. Alex Beam, a *Boston Globe* columnist who wrote the breezy *A Great Idea at the Time: The Rise, Fall, and Curious Afterlife of the Great Books*, observed of Adler's project, "There were no concessions to contemporary taste."[89] According to this line of reasoning, it is antidemocratic elitism for an insular coterie of academics to determine what books the masses ought to read before consulting modern interests. But is it not antidemocratic to dismiss, as the critics of the Great Books routinely do, the preferences of Ancient Athens, Medieval France, and Elizabethan England? That a book is still read hundreds of years after its publication date, and in languages foreign to its author, is a clue that it just might be a great book. But by looking past last night's Charlie Rose interview, last week's *New York Times* best-seller list, and last year's Modern Language Association panels, the Great Books offend the prisoner of his age. What does a Macedonian philosopher or a Victorian novelist have to say to a twenty-first-century American? The criticism mistakes proximity for profundity.

Snobbishness toward a movement that exposed middling minds to elite books strangely morphed into egalitarianism when confronted with the contention that very few books truly deserve the modifier "great." Why can't Rigoberta Menchú, Eldridge Cleaver, and Dan Brown be great too? Their popularity is parochial. It is mired in, rather than transcendent of, place and time. "The truth is that a fluency with the Great Books is no longer a prerequisite for professional or social success," Emily Eakin wrote in the *New York Times*. "Critical thinking skills arguably are. But those, some English professors are willing to admit, can be honed just as well through considerations of 'Sex and the City' as 'Middlemarch.'"[90] Kill your bookshelf. There is a rerun of *Cougar Town* to watch.

In the end, it was the populist nature of the Great Books project that soured cultural guardians. Snobs sought to disassociate themselves not from the books—though ultimately that they did—but from the uncouth people reading them. Know your place. There is Internet porn to surf, a txt 2 respond 2, and reality-show repeats to numb the brain. For many self-identified intellectuals, the cultural literacy bequeathed from reading Great Books was significant only as a mark of class separation. Now that every Tom, Dick, and Mary was reading works previously considered the best of the West, it was time to move on—and denigrate what was once praised. The sight of the fifty-four-volume set displayed in a parlor was enough to mark one as a rube. Better stock one's shelves with Foucault and Fanon if the point is acceptance among the poseur class.

A culture that discards the Great Books as passé is a culture in trouble. For highbrows, defining intellectual life by its distance from mainstream America is bad for them and for mainstream America. It isn't about the life of the mind but about status. For the masses, the void that once might have been filled by Great Books is filled by generally unfulfilling pursuits. The ramifications for society are disastrous. There are no literary common denominators. Separated from our heritage, we blindly march out of step into the future. More importantly, the demos of the democracy become the dunces of the dunceocracy. A populace educated by bread and circuses is less fit to govern than one educated by *The Republic* and *Hamlet*.

If the ruler, whether a king or 310 million people, is ill educated, God help the ruled. For Mortimer Adler the basic riddle of the American republic was: "How do we give the people of an industrial democracy the education that they need and deserve, which should be equivalent to the education which the small class—the ruling class—the leisure class—had in all the pre-industrial, undemocratic societies of the past?"[91] The answer was, as Matthew Arnold had famously written, through "the best which has been thought and said."[92]

Free-Market Evangelist
How a New Dealer–Turned–Libertarian
Taught the Everyman Economics

"During the Hutchins-Adler era," Milton Friedman recounted, "a favorite wisecrack was that the University of Chicago was a Baptist institution to which the good Presbyterians sent their children to be converted to Catholicism by a Jew."[1] The Great Books were not the only intellectual hotbed in midcentury Hyde Park.

In his memoirs, Milton Friedman described economics, which he studied at the Hutchins-Adler University of Chicago in the 1930s and taught there for thirty years beginning in 1946, as his life's vocation and public policy as his avocation.[2] Friedman's vocational success, winning a Nobel Prize and becoming arguably the most important economist of the twentieth century, owed much to the rich intellectual atmosphere of the University of Chicago economics department. His avocation's success in translating complex economic ideas to the common man, which is the concern of this chapter, found its roots within Friedman's roots.

The son of immigrants from Carpatho-Ruthenia, Milton Friedman was born in Brooklyn on July 31, 1912. About a year after his birth, his family moved to nearby Rahway, New Jersey. There the Friedmans lived atop their work. Their home ventures included a sweatshop clothing factory, a dry goods store, and an ice-cream parlor.

Friedman absorbed the entrepreneurialism. As a teenager, the future Nobelist scooped ice cream in his parents' shop and sold fireworks at a roadside stand. After landing a scholarship to Rutgers University, Friedman undertook numerous jobs and ventures that put him in the black during the Great Depression. He worked weekends as a department store clerk and lunches waiting tables. A meal served as pay for the latter job. As the lunch hour encroached on a European history course, the job bequeathed to Friedman the habit of quick eating and the only "C" on his college transcript. Capitalizing on a Rutgers tradition requiring freshmen to wear white socks and green ties, Friedman and a classmate bought the items wholesale and peddled them throughout the dormitories. The entrepreneurial duo later partnered with Barnes and Noble to buy used books from students at the end of the semester. They made 5 percent of what the bookstore paid out. Part of the deal included a provision allowing the young entrepreneurs the right to buy back books from Barnes and Noble at a discount. Having gleaned from professors their assigned readings for the following semester, Friedman and friend purchased those books from Barnes and Noble and made a killing reselling them. Other endeavors included teaching summer school and selling encyclopedias door to door.[3]

Rather than breed resentments, Friedman's experiences in the free market helped make him one of its most effective exponents. He trusted people to make their own decisions, and mistrusted elites to make decisions for them, because he knew both well. People were not *the masses*—a glob of humanity to be pushed in a singular direction by their superiors—but *individuals* with a multitude of interests unmanageable by remote. Friedman's economics never floated in the ether but instead remained grounded. He lectured his fellow economists that "the only relevant test of the *validity* of a hypothesis is comparison of its predictions with experience."[4]

Economics wasn't a parlor game. He infused common sense into his field—for example, pointing out that flooding the market with money, just as with widgets or apples, leads to depreciation. Friedman understood that economics wasn't merely about numbers. It was about people. Numbers are predictable; people—not so much. The variables, then, played havoc with the hubristic visions of planners. In his pamphlet *Roofs or Ceilings?*, in his book *Capitalism and Freedom*, in the pages of *Newsweek*, and in his television documentary *Free to Choose*, Friedman communicated not as a detached theorist but as one who knew the benefits of the market economy firsthand.

By directing this pamphlet, book, column, and television series at the intelligent masses from which he sprang, rather than staying in academia's intellectual ghetto, Friedman made a deeper impression on the twentieth century than all but a handful of human beings.

Birth of a Public Intellectual

In 1946, Milton Friedman the economist had his coming-out party as Milton Friedman the public intellectual. Along with George Stigler, Friedman authored *Roofs or Ceilings?* The pamphlet addressed the role federal rent controls played in the postwar housing shortage. The second in a series of pamphlets published by the Foundation for Economic Education (FEE), *Roofs or Ceilings?* gained a wider circulation of 500,000 through an abridged version distributed by the National Association of Real Estate Boards.

Friedman and Stigler's argument was fairly basic, though it ran against the grain of circa-1946 economics: Higher rents incentivize more economical use of available housing and stimulate demand for the construction of new units. Fixing rents below market value has the opposite consequence. Put simply, "The legal ceilings on rents are the reason there are so few places for rent."[5]

The publication of *Roofs or Ceilings?* was one of the most significant events in the history of American libertarianism. It highlighted Friedman's transition, then a work in progress, from New Deal liberalism to free-market capitalism. It set the template for his method of arguing from the opposition's point of view, which in the case of *Roofs or Ceilings?* may not have been radically different from his own. It introduced the economist to the dogmatic world of American libertarianism, where theoretical purity shouted down in-the-arena pragmatism. And it sparked several dramatic you're-dead-to-me splits among the heavyweights of American libertarianism.

Throughout *Roofs or Ceilings?*, the authors offered a Keynesian view of the source of inflation—ironic given their future monetarist reputations. The specific catalyst for the libertarian schism was a paragraph suggesting that the authors agreed with the notion that government should address income inequality, but that rent controls didn't address this issue at the source. Leonard Read, FEE's founder, suggested that the writers rethink the paragraph. They balked. Read attached an asterisked editorial note to the paragraph, diplomatically noting that "even from the standpoint of those who put equality above justice and liberty, rent controls are 'the height of folly.'"[6]

"We both regarded this note," Friedman explained of himself and his coauthor, "which in effect accused us of putting equality above justice and liberty, as inexcusable, and for some years we refused to have anything to do with the foundation or with Leonard Read."[7] Friedman wasn't the only one steamed. Ayn Rand, furious that FEE had anything to do with a pamphlet appealing to liberal sentimentalities, dubbed *Roofs or Ceilings?* "the most pernicious thing ever issued by an avowedly conservative organization." She forswore any future connection with FEE in an angry missive to Read.[8] And just as friendly fire besieged Read, Friedman and Stigler took flak from fellow academicians.[9]

Friedman's argumentation infuriated critics on the ends of the ideological spectrum. It also alleviated the acute massive housing shortage by helping to abolish the federal policy that had exacerbated the problem; the United States abandoned national rent control in 1949. The lessons were clear. Economics needn't be an abstract science divorced from people's lives. Persuasion trumped purity. Well-reasoned argument can topple a dominant ethos that is erected on a foundation of sand.

Capitalism and Freedom

In the late 1950s, Friedman delivered to an insular group of intellectuals a series of Volcker Fund–sponsored lectures that he would turn into a slim manifesto targeted toward the everyman reader. Whereas Friedman the economist was a one-man show, Milton and his wife were a package deal in his career as a public intellectual. Friedman noted that in his public-policy work, "Rose has been an equal partner, even with those publications, such as my *Newsweek* columns, that have been published under my name."[10] Credited on the title page of *Capitalism and Freedom* but not on the cover, Rose Friedman transformed the spoken lectures into content more fitting for the printed page.

On the eve of publication in 1962, Senator Barry Goldwater congratulated Friedman: "Professors sometimes have the habit of writing only for other professors, but your book is written in a way that the man on the street will understand and get your message."[11] It is this accessible style, buttressed by the authority of a University of Chicago economist, that sparked the sale of more than a half million copies.

Certainly it was not a courtier press. As Friedman noted in the foreword to the 1982 edition, the book was "so far out of the mainstream that it was not reviewed by any major national publication—not by the *New York Times* or the *Herald Tribune* (then still being published in New York) or the *Chicago Tribune*, or by *Time* or *Newsweek* or even the *Saturday Review*—though it was reviewed by the London *Economist* and by the major professional journals. And this for a book directed at the general public, written by a professor at a major U.S. university, and destined to sell more than 400,000 copies in the next eighteen years. It is inconceivable that such a publication by an economist of comparable professional standing but favorable to the welfare state or socialism or communism would have received a similar silent treatment."[12]

If Friedman could justly complain of reviewer indifference, he could at least hang his hat on a respectable publisher, albeit one who offered just a $1,500 advance.[13] Neither his friend Barry Goldwater's *Conscience of a Conservative* (Victor Publishing of Shepherdsville, Kentucky) nor mass-market offerings such as John Stormer's *None Dare Call It Treason* (Liberty Bell Press of Florissant, Missouri) or Phyllis Schlafly's *A Choice, Not an Echo* (Pere Marquette Press of Alton, Illinois) were embraced by mainstream publishers despite subsequently selling millions of copies. Many a right-wing author became a right-wing publisher in these years.

As George Nash notes in his history of postwar conservatism, *Capitalism and Freedom* was "one of the most significant works of conservative scholarship of the 1960s." One might add, with academia's increasingly partisan tilt, that it was one of the *only* works of conservative scholarship of the 1960s. "The publication of *Capitalism and Freedom* and Friedman's emergence as a preeminent economist among conservatives constituted a major landmark in the evolution of the postwar Right," explains Nash. "Here was a man of increasing prestige within his profession, a man whom even opponents respected as one of the very best American economists, who was articulating conservative viewpoints with a felicitous combination of learning and wit."[14]

Capitalism and Freedom expanded the parameters of debate by infusing respectability into causes previously deemed unworthy of respect. Friedman's book was published at the apex of postwar liberalism, and by tipping sacred cows it contributed to liberalism's rapid decline. The professor boldly pounced on supposedly untouchable programs, challenging paternalists to allow citizens the choice between private annuities and Social Security—ditto for the Post Office's monopoly over the mails. During the height of the New Frontier, he dissected President Kennedy's admonition, "Ask not what your country can do for you, ask what you can do for your country," as a statement that reflected the prevailing attitude—holding citizens as dependents in its first clause and, in its second, government as master. Abhorring racial discrimination, Friedman found the idea of forcing racially tolerant attitudes on homeowners and business proprietors inimical to property rights.[15] When he failed to convert opponents, he at least convinced them that such unpopular positions could be advanced through reason and not merely a grunt.

Capitalism and Freedom taught libertarians the limits to their ethic as it taught conservatives to limit their ethics. Friedman acknowledged that "freedom has nothing to say about what an individual does with his freedom; it is not an all-embracing ethic. Indeed, a major aim of the [classical] liberal is to leave the ethical problem for the individual to wrestle with."[16] This was less an indictment of liberty than of those who transgressed others' liberty in the name of virtue. "Those of us who believe in freedom must believe also in the freedom of individuals to make their own mistakes," Friedman cautioned. "Humility is the distinguishing virtue of the believer in freedom; arrogance, of the paternalist."[17]

The book engaged dominant liberalism in terms its votaries could understand and respect. Whereas Friedman advisee Barry Goldwater famously noted, "My aim is not to pass laws, but to repeal them," Friedman generally devised a good idea to compete with a bad one.[18] Milton Friedman wasn't born a right-winger. He didn't inherit the conservative "no" gene. As a New Dealer, for instance, he played an instrumental role in developing the Internal Revenue Service's "withholding" system of collecting taxes.[19] Though his orientation shifted from interventionist to libertarian, he retained the impulse to offer creative policy solutions to social questions. He didn't simply oppose. He offered alternatives, which made him a more engaging debating partner with interventionists. "He did not assume that his opponents were evil people," recalls Friedman's son, David. "So he didn't assume that what we have to do is fight them. He assumed what we have to do is to convince them."[20]

Nowhere was this more evident than in the discussion on public education. "Governments could require a minimum level of schooling financed by giving parents vouchers redeemable for a specified maximum sum per child per year if spent on 'approved' educational services," Friedman proposed. "Parents would then be free to spend this sum and any additional sum they themselves provided on purchasing educational services from an 'approved' institution of their own choice."[21] The GI Bill model, subsequently dubbed "school choice" or "vouchers," directed students toward the best rather than the closest school, forced underperforming schools to improve through competition, and ensured greater educational equality through greater parental autonomy. School choice became the cause of the Friedmans' lives, with the theory discussed in *Capitalism and Freedom* becoming practice, however limited in scope, in Cleveland, Milwaukee, and several other U.S. cities.[22]

Capitalism and Freedom showed that the politically free aren't fully free if they are economically directed. Friedman explained why intellectuals, who dream of assuming the role of planner in command economies, scoff at the importance of economic liberty: "Intellectuals in particular have a strong bias against regarding this aspect of freedom as important. They tend to express contempt for what they regard as material aspects of life, and to regard their own pursuit of allegedly higher values as on a different plane of significance and as deserving of special attention. For most citizens of the country, however, if not for the intellectual, the direct importance of economic freedom is at least comparable in significance to the indirect importance of economic freedom as a means to political freedom."[23] Democratic socialism is an oxymoron. Free enterprise is a means toward political liberty. The unmolested market is a check against political power.[24] Such heresies, rarely mouthed when *Capitalism and Freedom* was first published, became part of the political lexicon after its release.

Capitalism and Freedom highlighted the disconnect between the intentions of do-gooders and the atrocious results of their deeds. "Which if any of the great 'reforms' of past decades has achieved its objectives? Have the good intentions of the proponents of these reforms been realized?" In answer, Friedman produced a litany of policies that exacerbated the problems they sought to alleviate: "An income tax initially enacted at low rates and later seized upon as a means to redistribute income in favor of the lower classes has become a facade, covering loopholes and special provisions that render rates that are highly graduated on paper largely ineffective. . . . Monetary reforms, intended to promote stability in economic activity and prices, exacerbated inflation during and after World War I and fostered a higher degree of instability thereafter than had ever been experienced before. . . . A housing program intended to improve the housing conditions of the poor, to reduce juvenile delinquency, and to contribute to the removal of urban slums, has worsened the housing conditions of the poor, contributed to juvenile delinquency, and spread urban blight."[25] Policies, in other words, should be evaluated by ensuing reality and not dreams preceding.

Capitalism and Freedom marked a transition from Friedman the scholar to Friedman the public intellectual. A year after his inaugural book as a public intellectual, Friedman coauthored, with Anna Schwartz, *A Monetary History of the United States*, his last book-length work of economic scholarship. Certainly the University of Chicago professor would continue to make contributions to scholarship in lectures, articles, and other forums. But his focus was increasingly on influencing thought outside of academia. Friedman was already famous among economists. *Capitalism and Freedom* catapulted his fame among educated laymen.

Like a record that goes platinum without the benefit of airplay, *Capitalism and Freedom* sold hundreds of thousands of copies as an underground phenomenon shunned by cultural guardians. Bookstores were especially troublesome. "Except at college bookstores where Capitalism and Freedom was being assigned in a course, I have yet to find it available," the frustrated author reported to the paperback's publisher.[26] Other than the

Economist review, which found the book "ideal reading for politicians of either party" because it challenged conventional wisdom, reviewers stuck in conventional wisdom turned their backs.[27] So how did the ignored *Capitalism and Freedom* sell?

The University of Chicago professor's association with the Arizona senator who had become the hero of the resurgent Right propelled the book. When Goldwater, along with *Economics in One Lesson* author Henry Házlitt, endorsed the book, even the liberals at the University of Chicago Press had trouble containing their enthusiasm.[28] As Goldwater's presidential campaign gained traction, so did Friedman's book. *Business Week* reported that economists judged him "the logical candidate to become Goldwater's chief economic advisor," while *Newsweek* maintained that the economist might "do for Barry Goldwater what Galbraith once did for John F. Kennedy."[29] Friedman advising Goldwater sparked Goldwater's many fans to wonder just who this Friedman was.

For economists familiar with Friedman, the success of his accessible book encouraged them to make it required reading. "The Department of Economics has adopted the paperback Friedman, Capitalism and Freedom for use in our Principles of Economics course during the academic year of 1964–65," a Penn State professor explained to the publisher. "We anticipate an enrollment of 400 students for each of three terms. Would you have available in print this number of copies?"[30] With a dearth of texts by classical economists, a sympathy for balance or a sympathy for classical economics sparked professors to assign *Capitalism and Freedom*.

The book's mammoth sales prompted Friedman to name his Vermont retreat "Capitaf" in gratitude. The returns could not be quantified in mere royalties. *Capitalism and Freedom* also prompted the reluctant mainstream to come calling. Consequently, on question after question, Friedman would persuade the mainstream to reverse stream.

A Grand Forum

In the summer of 1966, *Newsweek* fired business columnist Henry Hazlitt, who had been with the magazine since its 1934 inception. The handpicked successor of H. L. Mencken at the *American Mercury* believed his conservative commentary had run afoul of the Graham family, who had purchased *Newsweek* earlier in the decade.[31] To replace Hazlitt's "Business Tides" column, the magazine hired a triumvirate of economists. Ironically, Milton Friedman, who had benefited so greatly from Hazlitt's endorsement of *Capitalism and Freedom*, was one of Hazlitt's replacements. Friedman alternated with left-wing MIT economist Paul Samuelson and middle-of-the-road future Federal Reserve governor Henry Wallich to write in the magazine's business section. The prospect of writing for a lay audience "scared" the professor. But at the urging of his wife, his son, and, ultimately, Henry Hazlitt, he accepted *Newsweek*'s offer. The gig paid $750 per column, or about $1 per word.[32]

Running in the September 26, 1966, issue, Friedman's first *Newsweek* column set the template for seventeen years' worth of columns that followed. Embracing a contrarian premise, Friedman bolstered his politically incorrect position with politically correct reasoning aimed at persuading, or perhaps infuriating, do-gooder readers. He played on left-wing emotions to buttress right-wing ideas. "Women, teen-agers, Negroes and particularly Negro teen-agers will be especially hit hard," Friedman explained about a minimum-wage hike. "I am convinced that the minimum-wage law is the most anti-Negro law on our statute books—in its effect not its intent."[33] Whether on Social Security, public schools, or subsidies to higher education, Friedman's take generally emphasized how such programs injured minorities, women, or the poor to the benefit of the rich and powerful. The initial article, like so many of his columns, provided a case study in how altruists hurt the very people they intend to help. As Friedman later quipped, "The true minimum wage rate is zero—the amount an unemployed person receives from his nonexistent employer."[34]

Friedman was a unique political animal: a practical libertarian. His success as a public intellectual stemmed from his refusal to bask in an ideological purity unsoiled by contact with the real world. Friedman's libertarianism was the stuff of public-policy concreteness rather than bull-session abstraction. This required as a starting point for any debate the recognition that the world was imperfect. School choice, for instance, didn't abolish public schools, as doctrinaire libertarians desired, but extended public aid to parents choosing private schools.[35] Friedman sought to reverse Fabianism through a reverse Fabianism, incrementally dismantling the welfare state that had been gradually erected. The notion of a negative income tax struck antistatists as anathema. Why should the government pay people for being poor? But if compared not against the ideal of limited government but with the reality of welfare's inefficiency, fraud, and penchant for ensnaring its recipients in dependency, then direct payments to poor individuals seemed preferable. In response to purist critics, he wrote that "dangers clearly exist" in embracing the lesser of two evils. "But they must be evaluated in terms of the world as it is, not in terms of a dream world in which there are no government welfare measures."[36]

Friedman's column was not an exercise in catharsis but a means of influencing public opinion and policy. In *Newsweek* he advocated floating exchange rates, ending the draft, abolishing wage and price controls, slashing tax rates, and legalizing the private ownership of gold before they became the policy of the United States. His influence was particularly profound among conservatives. In 1974, he used his *Newsweek* column to popularize a "new holiday [that] would celebrate our Personal Independence Day—the day in the year when we stop working to pay the expenses of government—Federal, state, and local—and start working to pay for the items we severally and individually choose in light of our own needs and desires."[37] Ever since, right-wingers have celebrated Tax Freedom Day.

When Friedman spoke, presidents not only listened—they repeated. Friedman wrote in *Newsweek* that "government is the problem, not the solution" more than eight years before Ronald Reagan famously said the same thing on his inauguration day.[38] One of Richard Nixon's most memorable lines—"We are all Keynesians now"—was Friedman recycled too, albeit out of its context.[39] Friedman practically wrote the playbook for the budgetary strategies of the Republican presidencies of 1980s and 2000s. In 1967, he warned, "If taxes are raised in order to keep down the deficit, the result is likely to be a higher norm for government spending. Deficits will again mount and the process will be repeated." He advised conservatives to "accept large deficits as the lesser of evils."[40]

Friedman was not averse to laying friendly fire down range at his former professor Arthur Burns, then chairman of the Federal Reserve, or two presidents whom he advised, Nixon and Reagan.[41] Even the most substantial free-market reform of his *Newsweek* tenure, the Kemp-Roth tax reduction, didn't escape his criticism (even as he supported the measure).[42]

Friedman's independent voice often infuriated readers disposed to agree with him. One of his first columns, for instance, condemned the draft as "inequitable, wasteful and inconsistent with a free society"—a theme he would return to long after the Nixon administration had abolished conscription, in large part because of his efforts.[43] When Friedman blasted advertising restrictions on tobacco as contrary to the First Amendment, an Indiana reader responded: "And then there is the narcotics law. You could argue, as you do about smoking, that this is a 'divisible' issue, and that some persons might want to enjoy their narcotics even though they will die much sooner. Yet I doubt you would want to abolish the narcotics laws."[44] But that is where his logic took him. Friedman wrote in 1972 that "we have no right to use force, directly or indirectly, to prevent a fellow from committing suicide, let alone from drinking alcohol or taking drugs."[45] A principled consistency strangely made him unpredictable among readers used to columnists enlisting in the scrivener's auxiliary of one of the two major parties.

Friedman's most controversial column discussed abolishing governmental barriers to drug use, a step that even the most libertine hippies shied away from. The columnist asked readers to play a bureaucrat faced with making two mistakes. The first involved approving a drug that resulted in deaths, injury, and illness. The second involved blocking a drug that could save and improve lives. "If you make the first mistake, the results will be emblazoned on the front pages of the newspapers," Friedman wrote. "If you make the second mistake, who will know it?" In other words, the CYA mentality that governs bureaucratic behavior inevitably results in lives lost. Friedman advocated repealing the stringent standards for Food and Drug Administration (FDA) approval of drugs, and put to print the heretical thought that Americans might be better off without an FDA.[46]

The column unleashed a barrage of criticism, including a series of defensive articles in the *Washington Post* and hearings held by Senator Gaylord Nelson.[47] "I never thought I would ever write a 'Dear Sir, You cur!' letter to you," a "warm admirer" responded. "I was shocked at the amount of casuistry, sophistry, ignoring of telling truths, and half-truths that you managed to pack into one page."[48] The controversy sparked a follow-up column, "Barking Cats," which its author rightly regarded as one of his best.[49] In response to a scientist who accepted criticisms of the FDA but still deemed the agency necessary, Friedman rhetorically asked: "What would you think of someone who said, I would like to have a cat, provided it barked?" This illogical "barking cat" mentality governed the responses of letter writers who wished for an FDA, just not one that stifled new medicine. "The way the FDA now behaves, and the adverse consequences, are not an accident, not a result of some easily corrected human mistake, but a consequence of its constitution in precisely the same way that a meow is related to the constitution of a cat. As a natural scientist, you recognize that you cannot assign characteristics at will to chemical and biological entities, cannot demand that cats bark or water burn. Why do you suppose that the situation is different in the social sciences?"[50]

Though Friedman's independent streak certainly endeared him to *Newsweek*'s editors, he did not play the role of house conservative. In 1967, the columnist blasted *Newsweek* for its lengthy "Negro in America" cover story that listed numerous factors impeding progress for African Americans but overlooked the role of minimum-wage laws in excluding blacks from the labor force.[51] Friedman's clashes with the magazine generally happened outside his readers' view. When he wrote a piece attacking the magazine *in the magazine*, his editor playfully responded with a contract extension. Friedman then attacked the editor's implicit assumption that tolerance was a characteristic of liberals. "Here again liberals have tended to take the word for the deed," he wrote in a letter. "They profusely profess tolerance yet I know from extensive experience that they frequently do not practice it."[52] Two years into his tenure, he demanded his paymasters double his salary, which left his editor "frankly a bit startled" but he eventually persuaded *Newsweek* to increase Friedman's pay by about half.[53] In a 1968 note labeled *"Personal and Not for Publication,"* Friedman, in characteristically blunt fashion, complained to editor Larry Martz: "The enclosed item on the negative income tax in your Periscope of May 6 is incompetent reporting."[54] Ten years later, he wrote Martz on a California ballot initiative limiting taxation: "I have been very much disturbed by the incredibly low quality of *Newsweek*'s reporting on Proposition 13," calling his employer's journalism "full of mistakes," "disgraceful," and "little short of out and out propaganda."[55]

Ultimately, though a public intellectual, Friedman was an economist, and not just any economist but a monetary economist of the Chicago School. Over the course of seventeen years worth of columns, most, to one degree or another, addressed monetary policy—perhaps the least understood aspect of economic policy. The timing of Friedman's emergence as a public intellectual in *Newsweek* couldn't have been more fortuitous. His tenure with the magazine roughly overlapped with one of the more unstable periods for the dollar. A subject considered dry when noticed at all suddenly became de rigueur in the inflationary era. Economics, as Brian Domitrovic writes in *Econoclasts*, was "becoming something of a national pastime. For in the early 1970s, the economy began to fail badly, and people wanted answers."[56]

The ridicule meeting Friedman's 1967 prediction of an inflationary recession, flying in the face of the prevailing Keynesianism, only added to his legend as events unhappily proved him correct.[57] If his phrase "inflationary recession" failed to catch on, the concept did in the term "stagflation," which would be on every pundit's lips in the 1970s. Before events disproved the Phillips Curve, Milton Friedman did. One needn't sacrifice inflation for employment, or vice versa. Monetarism, Friedman informed his lay audience, is scientific rather than ideological; it "has little to say about fiscal policy, government policy toward industry or the long-term rate of growth of the economy. Bad monetary policy can destroy a healthy economy but good monetary policy cannot by itself cure a sick economy."[58]

Friedman found inflation so insidious because it stealthily pushed Americans into higher tax brackets, played havoc with interest rates, and enabled politicians to finance the growth of government without paying a price for it. Friedman rebuffed both the gold bugs on the Right and the tinkerers on the Left. Regarding the latter, "We simply do not know enough—or, equivalently, the economy is too complex and variable—for us to be able to manipulate the fine-tuning dials with enough precision to get the desired results. We end up instead introducing additional disturbances to the economy."[59] Friedman favored a course of steady expansion of the money supply to reflect economic and population growth.

When homemakers descended upon supermarkets to protest rising prices in 1966, Friedman wrote, "Housewives have a justifiable complaint. But they should complain to Washington where inflation is produced, not to the supermarket where inflation is delivered."[60] In the simplest terms possible to readers who would understand it in no other way, Friedman explained, "Inflation is always and everywhere a monetary phenomenon," and, "Inflation is made in Washington and can only be eliminated in Washington."[61] Interspersed with such easy-to-grasp slogans were complex formulae, such as M1 and M2, more often found in academic journals than in glossy newsweeklies. Friedman's *Newsweek* column was a compromise in which the writer descended from the ivory tower and the reader ascended above the mass.

By late 1983, Friedman's columns appeared erratically. "I have always tried to make my column as topical as possible," he wrote to *Newsweek* editor William Broyles Jr. "I cannot do that if I do not know whether the column will appear next week, two weeks later, or three weeks later. I do not want to write columns for cold storage." Fix the problem, or get a new columnist, Friedman told his editor.[62] But Broyles was on his way out. Within two weeks of the ultimatum, Richard M. Smith had taken over the reins of the magazine. The squeaky wheel, rather than getting the grease, got rolled to the curb. The new editor explained that he wanted business columns that reported rather than analyzed.[63]

Friedman inaccurately predicted a recession in his January 16, 1984, column, meaning that the columnist who had come into *Newsweek* with a bang would part with a whimper.[64] Rather than announce Friedman's departure, the new editor blunted any backlash by keeping the popular economist's name on the masthead even as he kept his column out of the magazine. Though disturbed by the "disingenuousness," Friedman accepted payment from the magazine as his name appeared on the masthead for the next six months.[65] Readers eventually caught on.

Friedman missed the grand forum, but not the hard deadlines.[66] Though he continued to write for mass-market publications, most notably for the *Wall Street Journal*, he did so without the regularity of the triweekly *Newsweek* column that he enjoyed from 1966 until 1984.

Free to Choose

In 1977, the Public Broadcasting Service (PBS) aired a thirteen-part series articulating the economic philosophy of John Kenneth Galbraith. It wasn't merely that *The Age of Uncertainty* was unbalanced; it was redundant. Hadn't PBS viewers heard this message before? The conventional program sparked an unconventional local public television executive to plot a response truer to PBS's spirit of televising fare that could not be found elsewhere.

"I really would love to produce a counterprogram," Robert Chitester, the president of a tiny public television station in Erie, Pennsylvania, told Allen Wallis, a former classmate of Friedman's who then headed the Corporation for Public Broadcasting.

"If you really are serious, Bob, I know who should host the program," Wallis responded.

Who?

"Milton Friedman."

"I am certain I did not know who that was," recalls Chitester.[67]

Chitester came to know Friedman through *Capitalism and Freedom*, a book he soon adopted as his "Bible."[68] Then he came to know Friedman in early 1977 through four visits to San Francisco, where the sixty-five-year-old had retired. The western trips were aimed not so much at persuading Milton to do the program as at persuading his wife to give her imprimatur. "My challenge was to get Rose comfortable that she could trust the integrity of what I was saying," notes Chitester. Apart from gaining the trust of Milton's guard dog, Chitester faced the added obstacle of his ostensible ally PBS, which lobbied Friedman not to work with the maverick broadcaster.[69]

The stars aligned for Milton Friedman's transition from the classroom to the small screen. In late 1976, the Swedish Academy of Science awarded him the Nobel Memorial Prize in Economics. Friedman's retirement from the University of Chicago that same year allowed new challenges. His stature had never been greater. His time had never been freer.

"Providing that the funding is assured, I am prepared to devote a large part of my time and energies during the next year to 18 months to a TV series designed to present my personal social, economic and political philosophy," Friedman wrote Chitester in July 1977, confirming what he had told him earlier that year. "Our understanding is that you will have primary managerial responsibility and control and that I will have final editorial control."[70]

The project sought to bring *Capitalism and Freedom* to television. Working titles included *Capitalism and Freedom*, *The Invisible Hand*, *Friedman on Freedom*, *In Pursuit of Freedom*, and *Free: Free to Choose* until producer Michael Latham's *Free to Choose* stuck and won him a champagne bounty.[71] Chitester and Friedman originally envisioned basing the documentary on lectures, whose best bits would be surrounded by interesting visuals emphasizing Friedman's points. The lectures, later marketed as *Milton Friedman Speaks*, provided many ideas upon which Friedman based the outline and narration of *Free to Choose*. But straight lectures, however dynamic the lecturer, did not lend themselves to a ten-hour miniseries competing with the likes of *The Jeffersons*, *One Day at a Time*, and *Fantasy Island*. Viewers, even in the protocable era, were free to choose. The project demanded something more ambitious and visually arresting.

Funding such an endeavor would require in excess of three million dollars, more than the annual budget of Chitester's Erie television station. With the zeal of a convert, and without the financial backing of PBS, the McGovernite-turned-Friedmanite enthusiastically ventured hat-in-hand into Corporate America.

"I'm visiting Lilly Endowment, Ransburg Corporation, Hallmark Cards and FMC Corporation next week," Chitester wrote to Friedman more than two years from air date. "I've sent material to George Eccles in Salt Lake City, and very strong follow-up letters to Peter Grace, Donald Kendall, Fritz Jewett (Potlatch), Bernard Frazer (Firestone), and Fluor Corporation. I've talked with T. C. at Starr Foundation, and unfortunately the estate is still not settled. I'm planning meetings with General Mills and General Motors as soon as another 'major' corporate grant is made."[72]

"I was constantly sleeping on airplanes, flying on airplanes, going everywhere," Chitester remembers. "It was hectic."[73]

Because of the ambitious scope of the series, PBS waived rules that normally limited major donors to seven. Chitester could solicit donations from fifteen underwriters. That still meant Chitester needed to raise an average of $235,000 from each donor. Getty Oil, Pepsico, Firestone, General Motors, and W. R. Grace were among the megacorporations that funded the series, along with such conservative philanthropies as the Sarah Scaife Foundation and the John M. Olin Foundation.[74]

In 1977, Friedman chose British-based Video Arts as his production company. The principals—Milton, Rose, and David Friedman, producer Michael Latham, WQLN's Bob Chitester, economist Ben Rogge, and Anthony Jay, Michal Peacock, and Robert Reid from Video Arts—convened in Boston from November 22 to 25 to lay the groundwork for the series. The group selected ten ideas on which to base their ten programs, and decided on "Who Will Protect the Consumer?" as the pilot.[75]

Friedman laid down the law, actually four of them, to the producers. First, there would be no gimmicks.

Second, the series would be "open and unashamedly" intellectual. Third, viewers would be sacrificed for high-mindedness. And finally, he wouldn't play dummy to even the most skilled ventriloquist; the words he spoke would be his own.[76]

Tony Jay suggested "para-autobiography" as a mechanism to propel the miniseries: "Milton could take episodes in his life and his studies that revealed progressively the evidence that has led to his conclusions."[77] A series that relied on personal anecdotes rather than objective facts horrified Friedman. "My personal reaction, to speak quite frankly, is to cringe as I read the successive highly personal introductions," he explained to his British producers. "That is simply not me." He hoped for a documentary that appealed to the viewer's "reason rather than emotion." To Friedman, whoring out his rags-to-riches story seemed the flipside of ad hominem argumentation.[78] With a few exceptions, *Free to Choose* remained true to his vision of a program that said much about Milton Friedman's philosophy but little about Milton Friedman.

The filming took Friedman to Adam Smith's haunts at the University of Glasgow, to a boat in Hong Kong's bustling harbor, inside a Federal Reserve Bank's gold vault, to a primitive Indian weaving village, and to points beyond. Friedman provided on-camera narration, and voiceovers, remarkably without a script. As he later explained to a correspondent, "My forte is spontaneous talk, not reading written text. Hence, he [Michael Latham] agreed with my outlandish suggestion that there should be no script for the film."[79] For a few takes that actually made it into the film, he stumbled over his words. But the verbal mishaps merely reminded viewers that they had tuned in for the world's most influential economist, not a polished television presenter.

Those making the case for the free market most compellingly were often not Friedman but the interviewed subjects. The human-interest vignettes conveyed the important point that economics wasn't about numbers. It was about people—people like Manchester, England's Mark Ramsay, who remained on the dole for seven years rather than work for comparable pay; Rochester, New York's Patricia Brennan, whose mail delivery service was shut down by the government's monopoly; and Las Vegas, Nevada's Lance von Allmen, who gambled all on his dream to make millions from his antipollution "oil eater" product.[80] These were living, rather than numeric, symbols of economic principles—incentives versus disincentives, competition, and profit and loss. Black-and-white statistics couldn't convey the point the way flesh and blood could.

Friedman had long objected to television on pedagogical grounds. He contended that anybody who could be converted in a thirty-minute sitting wasn't worth converting, since the next program could just as easily recapture.[81] The written word, not the idiot box, held the key to persuasion. But *Free to Choose* demonstrated that the publishing medium, like television, had limitations. Friedman walking through the rubble of abandoned Bronx apartment buildings told the story of how rent control compelled landlords to abandon unprofitable property. The visual of the tiny professor surrounded by giant stacks of the *Federal Register* conveyed the byzantine nature of the regulatory code. The monetarist halting the Treasury's money press literally demonstrated how inflation is stopped.[82] These were luxuries that *Free to Choose* the book simply didn't have.

Location filming ended on November 20, 1978. *Free to Choose* featured a discussion session immediately following each half-hour documentary that highlighted Friedman's debating skills, saved money, and presented dissenting views to public television aficionados skittish about free enterprise. Recorded at the University of Chicago's Harper Library in September 1979, and moderated by University of London sociologist Bob McKenzie, the discussions featured leading thinkers on the issues highlighted in the preceding documentary.

No doubt the respondents vocalized the responses of many PBS viewers. "This film has set me on edge," conceded Richard Deason, a leader of the International Brotherhood of Electrical Workers, regarding "Who Protects the Worker?" "From Cradle to Grave" prompted James Dumpson, a former New York City welfare administrator, to admit: "As I looked at the film, I had a growing sense of anger." A seething Frances Fox Piven repeatedly invoked Chile—where Friedman had controversially held a short meeting with Augusto Pinochet in 1975—in non sequitur fashion in the conversation following "Created Equal."[83] But on the whole, Friedman encountered not opprobrium but counterarguments. The producers selected Friedman's foils to effectively rebut his arguments, not to play straw men. Contra the verbal food fights of today's cable talk, the conversation of the likes of *The Other America* author Michael Harrington, former Fed chairman William McChesney Martin, and MIT economist Jagdish Bhagwati ensured measured discussions in which competing positions were clearly articulated and not distorted amidst the din. In all but one of the discussions, the opposition outnumbered Friedman.

Public television seemed a strange venue for Milton Friedman's ideas. "I have strongly, and for long, been opposed to government subsidies for PBS," Friedman explained to incredulous journalists covering the launch of *Free to Choose*. "I do not think there should be government appropriations for PBS."[84] Friedman had earned a state scholarship to Rutgers, lived in a rent-controlled apartment while teaching at Chicago, and gladly taken government grants as he advocated their abolition.[85] He embraced his contradictions, announcing in his memoirs that "the New Deal was a lifesaver for us personally. The new government programs created a boom market for economists, especially in Washington. Absent the New Deal, it is far from clear that we could have gotten jobs as economists."[86]

All this made him a hypocrite to his adversaries. But to Friedman it was merely an acknowledgment that he lived in the world rather than in his dream world. As he cautioned an Ivy League economist inspired to forgo government grants by his arguments for abolishing the National Science Foundation, "We are members of a society; we live by the rules of that society; we participate in the making of those rules; we win some, lose more, but there is nothing wrong if we are in the minority in acting individually so as to promote our own interests."[87] In other words, don't deny yourself benefits just because you philosophically disagree with their existence.

Friedman took flak for taking advantage of a system he railed against. He took flak for participating in the capitalist system that he advocated. "There are a lot of different ways to get your dose of Milton Friedman these days," *Fortune* magazine reported. "Besides his regular column in *Newsweek* and the television series, there is a new book, called *Free to Choose* ($9.95), video

cassettes of the TV series ($4,800), the same ten pro-
grams on 16-mm film ($6,200), and fifteen videotaped
lectures called 'Milton Friedman Speaks' ($500 for one
lecture and $7,000 for them all)."[88]

The commercialism struck Friedman as distasteful.
He told Michael Peacock two years before air date that
"enough is enough." "I feel embarrassed at the prospect of
using the same material so many ways in so many different
forms," he wrote, anticipating *Fortune*'s criticism of him.
"There are first of all the lectures; second, the transcripts
of the lectures plus the study guides accompanying them;
third, the television program itself; fourth, the book that
Rose and I will be doing as an update of Capitalism and
Freedom to accompany the lecture program. It is hard to
justify still a fifth retelling of the same material."[89]

How much did Friedman bank? Characteristically
cantankerous, the economist told *Fortune*, "It's none of
your damn business."[90] It was Friedman's business, and a
quite profitable one at that. Set at $100,000, Friedman's
fee for the ten-part series was based on his $10,000 lec-
ture fee, the rationale being that each show would be
judged the equivalent of a lecture. Chitester, foresee-
ing the project as more ambitious than that simplistic
analysis allowed, ultimately increased Friedman's fee by
half.[91] The book based on the series became the third
best-selling hardcover nonfiction book of 1980.[92]

Viewers implored Friedman to run for president.[93]
A Missouri couple was "chagrined to realize that not
everyone in the nation watched it. In fact we know that
of our friends maybe 2 of 10 have the sense to watch your
programs rather than the Dukes of Hazzard."[94] Yet rat-
ings exceeded expectations. About three million people
viewed each episode of the public television miniseries in

the United States, with *Free to Choose* finding its way onto the British, Japanese, and German airwaves.[95] Another viewer lauded *Free to Choose* for providing "hope that there is really an underlying grass-roots sentiment in this country that is capable of turning the country around."[96]

When *Free to Choose* aired in the second week of 1980, inflation approached 14 percent in the United States. America had just endured a year of idling cars waiting in long lines for gasoline. The brazen aggression of the Soviet Union invading Afghanistan the month prior to premiere symbolized a decline of the West vis-à-vis the Eastern Bloc. The president seemed resigned to malaise as a permanent condition.

America was sick and tired of being sick and tired. Tax revolts, notably Howard Jarvis's Proposition 13 in California and Barbara Anderson's Proposition 2 ½ in Massachusetts, constrained the ability of politicians to enlarge government coffers by shrinking citizens' wallets. Ronald Reagan's election in 1980 inaugurated an era of deregulation, tighter money, and tax cuts. The 70 percent top marginal income tax rate that prevailed in 1981 was felled to 28 percent before Reagan left office. The economy, unsurprisingly, reacted by expanding for more than seven years, and, if not for a brief downturn in 1990–91, for nearly two decades. Inflation, which peaked at 14.8 percent in March 1980, dipped to 1.1 percent by December 1986. Inflation simply ceased being an issue of political salience. Though Reagan's landslide election signaled the beginning of something new, many of the beneficial changes actually predated his victory. Tight-money man Paul Volcker, selected to head the Fed by Jimmy Carter, came closer to approximating Friedman's monetary ideas than did his predecessors. The deregulation of the airlines and trucking industry began under Carter, as did the challenge to Ma Bell's status as the state-sanctioned telephone monopoly. The times, more so than any officeholder, dictated change.

Free to Choose benefited from this zeitgeist. *Free to Choose* helped create this zeitgeist.

Friedman's World

Milton Friedman died on November 19, 2006. It's telling that the best tributes came from adversaries rather than allies. Former Harvard president and U.S. treasury secretary Lawrence Summers eulogized him in the *New York Times* by opining that "any honest Democrat will admit that we are now all Friedmanites." Friedman, he conceded, "has had more influence on economic policy as it is practiced around the world today than any other modern figure."[97] Paul Krugman, a fellow Nobelist and fierce critic of Friedman, dubbed him "one of the most important economic thinkers of all time, and possibly the most brilliant communicator of economic ideas to the general public that ever lived." Krugman granted, "By any measure—protectionism versus free trade; regulation versus deregulation; wages set by collective bargaining and government minimum wages versus wages set by the market—the world has moved a long way in Friedman's direction."[98]

Part of the reason is that Milton Friedman lived in the real world that other economists theorized about from a distance. John Maynard Keynes, the only twentieth-century economist rivaling Friedman's import, was educated at Eton and Cambridge, which are about as far away from Rahway as it gets. Friedman waited tables, peddled socks door-to-door, and manned roadside fireworks stands. He attended the public schools and lived in rent-controlled apartments. His brilliant mind was buttressed by experience.

There is still a state post office, an FDA, and government television. Drugs remain largely illegal. Poor children continue to be condemned to dreadful noneducations in the public school monopoly. And Friedman's pragmatism-over-purity approach has more than once resulted in blowback. Proponents of such statist policies as emissions trading, the earned-income tax credit, and the motorist congestion tax cite Friedman's ideas as inspiration.[99] But much of what Milton Friedman intentionally advocated, precisely because he served as advocate, has come to pass.

The U.S. government doesn't fix prices, doesn't confiscate privately owned gold, doesn't order men into its army. Top marginal tax rates are less than half of what they were when Friedman called for their reduction in *Capitalism and Freedom*. Entire industries, such as airlines, telephone, and trucking, have been deregulated, as his *Newsweek* column demanded. The inflation menace has been tamed as a direct result of Friedman's tireless efforts. Friedman's influence outside of his homeland is even more profound. European Communism has fallen, with *Free to Choose* serving as a guidebook to fledgling market economies in Estonia and Mongolia.[100] Trade has become liberalized. Markets, rather than governments, determine exchange rates. The economist was no prophet outlining the future, but a wiseman guiding us there.

It's Milton Friedman's world. We just live in it.

4

The Longshoreman Philosopher
How an Unschooled Hobo Became
a Favorite of Presidents and Prime Time

Bob Chitester, fresh from producing *Free to Choose*, thought it a great idea to connect two of the era's great minds: Milton Friedman and Eric Hoffer. With both living a few miles from one another in San Francisco, the pair seemed easy enough to bring together. But when Hoffer took Chitester's call—as usual, at a pay phone at a designated hour—he declined the offer. Hoffer was characteristically the solitary man, and he believed Friedman an ideologue of the kind he had often written about.[1] The longshoreman philosopher surely preferred the company of other workingmen to a Nobel Prize winner, even when the Nobel Prize winner arose from similarly humble origins.

"If ever there was a walking advertisement for the Great Books approach to education," Thomas Sowell writes, "it was Eric Hoffer."[2] The longtime dockworker was the definitional autodidact. Without even a grade school education, Hoffer taught himself the classics by patronizing used-book stores and public libraries throughout California. The road was his study. America became his classroom.

Hoffer's earliest memories revolve around his father's books. At five, he would sort them according to color, size, language, weight. He taught himself to read both English and German. Then tragedy struck. Carrying young Eric down the stairs, his mother slipped. The fall eventually resulted in the dainty mother's death and her oversized son's blindness and amnesia. A German maid, Martha Bauer, raised the blind boy. At fifteen, Eric miraculously regained his sight. With the threat of losing his vision constant, Eric devoured every book on which he placed hands. Then, in 1920, tragedy struck again. His cabinetmaker-intellectual father died. With three hundred dollars from the cabinetmakers guild, Eric, like so many Americans wanting to begin anew, went west.

On the Road

"Logic told me that California was the poor man's country," the Bronx-bred Hoffer recalled. "And so I landed in Los Angeles in the early nineteen twenties. I had several trunks full of things and books. I rented a room not far from the public library and lived from day to day."[3] In the Golden State, Hoffer figured he could sleep outside and pick his next meal from the nearest orange tree.[4] When money dried up, he gravitated to skid row. When hope ran out, he decided to check out.

He consulted *Encyclopedia Britannica* on poison and bought the supplies for a quarter. "I poured the oxalic crystals into a bottle half full of water," Hoffer recalled a half century later. "Part of it dissolved and the rest settled on the bottom. I wrapped the bottle in a newspaper and went out beyond the city, where any cries of anguish would find no response, and if, driven by pain, I would rush back for help it would be of no avail, for a run of two miles or so would accelerate the working of the poison and put an end to all efforts." There, nobody but Eric Hoffer could save Eric Hoffer. He spit up the concoction upon tasting it.[5]

"I did not commit suicide, but on that Sunday a workingman died and a tramp was born."[6] For ten years, from late 1931 until Pearl Harbor, Hoffer lived a hand-to-mouth existence. He prospected for gold in the Sierra Nevadas. He picked cotton, hops, tomatoes, apples, and berries up and down California. He wintered in Berkeley, where he bused tables on Shattuck Avenue. He hopped trains and sported library cards throughout the state. He romanced high-class ladies and street whores. He made no permanent friendships.[7]

"Late in January 1934 I found myself in San Diego[,] California, penniless and with no job in sight," Hoffer recalled. "I had been roaming the state following the crops and working at odd jobs. It was an inexpensive and, to me, pleasant existence." Hoffer spotted a vegetable truck. He began unloading its contents and "devouring cabbage cow-fashion." Two foodless days will have that bovine effect on a man. It will also make a tramp reconsider, at least temporarily, the settled existence. The truck driver permitted the transient to hitch a ride 180 miles east. In El Centro, Hoffer enrolled in a New Deal work camp that provided food, a shower, clothes, smokes, a bed, recreation, and four dollars a month. He dug ditches for gas and water pipes for government homes near El Centro. He created firebreaks in the San Bernardino Mountains. He laid rock for walkways, walls, and steps at its Del Rosa ranger station. He fought fires at Big Bear. Whereas the El Centro camp was a lazy "human junk yard" of cripples, drunks, and the elderly, San Bernardino's camp, though comprised of the same troubled stock, provided an orderly and efficient environment that Hoffer believed unleashed feats from the men far beyond the expected.[8]

"It was my first experience of life in close contact with a crowd. To eat, sleep and spend the greater part of the day with two hundred strange human beings was something new and disquieting. I lacked even the rudiments of sociability."[9] He tentatively interacted. He ebulliently watched. The social handicap bestowed observational strengths. People were alien to his native habitat. So the wanderer noticed traits about humans that humans accustomed to humans overlooked. He marveled at man's propensity to exaggerate and to argue through dogmatic statements instead of reason. He described a trio of men consulting a book on numerology to determine their destined trades by "manipulating their dates of birth" and noticed the prevalence of mangled hands among men like him. The observations ranged from the profound to the mundane, with the banal occasionally appearing prophetic in hindsight. "My days in the camps were full of discoveries and new impressions. These discoveries were, probably not so much of transients as of human beings, and most of the observations might be true of any group of average people brought together by chance anywhere in the U.S."[10]

He knew people. He knew himself. He spent a few months in a camp and then moved on. "To have a few nickels and to tramp the roads which stretch into nowhere, seemed the height of pleasure."[11]

Behind one of the most original books of the twentieth century lay the story of an American original. Or did it?

The Invention of Eric Hoffer

"All we know about his early life is what Hoffer chose to tell us," Tom Bethell points out.[12] What Hoffer told us makes such a compelling tale that his life story, often repeated, was never questioned. On the dust jackets of his books, in newspaper profiles, and in television introductions, Hoffer's fans invariably came across the Dickensian narrative involving blindness and then miraculous sight, parental loss, skid row, and life on the bum. Everybody who had encountered Hoffer in these unforgettable years had apparently forgotten him. No single person who knew him before fame found him on the San Francisco waterfront came forward to say that they knew him way back when.

Just as he had escaped the memories of acquaintances during these first four decades, Hoffer escaped the state's notice. He bequeathed no birth certificate, diplomas, selective service papers, or passport for researchers to inspect. Hoffer lived off the grid. The last free American, Hoffer fired his employers at will, moved on a whim, and played the invisible man to the all-seeing state. It is the mystery of Eric Hoffer, as much as the myth, which fascinates us. Like the Hoffer that appeared to friends, the Hoffer that appears to history is a guarded figure telling some, hiding some. Like those who knew him, we will never truly know him. Naturally, since we want to know what we do not know, we want to know Eric Hoffer.

In 1937, the wanderer's existence was independently verified. He revealed himself by filling out a Social Security application. But the state's affirmation of his existence only adds to the mystery. Rather than the 1902 birth he later officially maintained, Hoffer listed his date of birth as July 25, 1898. Why would he later subtract four years from his life? Perhaps he sought to join the fight in World War II or obscure not joining it in World War I. Maybe the age reduction helped a fortysomething sans experience gain admission to the longshoreman's union. Did the auguries of numerology influence him to manipulate his birth date along with the men he observed in the New Deal camp? "He wanted to be part of this century, and not of the past," theorized Lili Osborne, his longtime companion.[13]

As he wanted to be of the present and not the past, Hoffer wanted to be a man of the New World and not the Old. Allegedly born in the Bronx to German immigrants from Alsace, he spoke with a heavy European accent that seemed to migrate among Germany, Spain, and Italy, which appeared to give his expressive hands their permanent dialect. Could that foreign accent have come from the Bronx? "That's what he said," Osborne dryly commented. "Theoretically, he was born in the Bronx."[14]

And what of his dramatic tale of sight lost and then regained? "He told stories," his companion playfully explained. "How much do you believe in stories?"[15]

But Hoffer's greatest creation was not his life story. It was a slim book.

The Stevedore Socrates

"I find that in order to feel well both mentally and physically I have to write a certain number of words each day," Hoffer noted five years before the publication of *The True Believer*. "It is of no importance to get to the root of this necessity. It is a fact—a fortunate fact—and should be given full consideration."[16] Starting in the 1930s, after mining Montaigne during a winter venture in gold prospecting, reader Hoffer became writer Hoffer. He penned two unpublished novels, a biographical sketch of life on the bum, and, most significantly for his literary future, punchy observations about human behavior.

A year after revealing himself to the government, Hoffer revealed himself to the literary world. In 1938, the itinerant worker submitted a letter to *Common Ground*, a magazine aimed at American immigrants (like himself?). Margaret Anderson, the assistant to the editor, informed Hoffer that they could not print his lengthy missive. The rejection letter proved one of the most fruitful in publishing history. Anderson served as an informal literary adviser and emotional booster to Hoffer for the remainder of their days. She sent Hoffer's letter to Harper & Brothers, the firm that, in its various incarnations, subsequently published all of his books. The publishing house encouraged Hoffer to pen an autobiography, which didn't interest him. But Anderson's "goading hand," as Hoffer reported in the dedication of his first book, pushed Hoffer to write when he might have lost faith.[17] Anderson served as Hoffer's literary confidante from across a continent. Like everybody else, she barely knew him.

Hoffer's coworkers knew him enough to nickname him "the professor."[18] But most did not know him enough to know his last name. Rejected for military service, the fortysomething Hoffer became a dockworker in 1942 to aid the war effort. Though he undoubtedly served the Allied cause, Hoffer, a thinker shaped by revulsion to the totalitarian '30s, joined a union that had undermined America and served the interests of Hitler and Stalin during the pair's no-honor-among-thieves pact. The future scourge of joiners joined the International Longshoremen's and Warehousemen's Union (ILWU), the Harry Bridges–led outfit known for pushing the extremist politics of the Communist Party functionary at its head.[19] Hardly a mouthpiece for Hoffer's beliefs (or many of its other members' beliefs for that matter), the ILWU nevertheless served as a surrogate family and guarantor of a steady income. Hoffer proved a reliable member: manning picket lines, sporting an ILWU button, and attending tedious union meetings. But he did so as follower and not leader, listener and not speaker, cog and not engineer.

If Hoffer's intellectual pursuits, to the extent that they were fully known, struck fellow stevedores as odd, stranger still was his continued work on the waterfront long after his literary success. Until union regulations forced him into retirement in 1967, he worked several days a week as a longshoreman. Even as presidents and literary critics feted him, he kept loading DDT bound for India and unloading asbestos from East Africa. He broke ribs, busted toes, and crushed a thumb, which required amputation and a Dr. Frankenstein–like reconstruction. Such trials served as acid tests intensifying Hoffer's commitment to work on the San Francisco docks.[20] "I must feel that I am first and last a working-man and not a thinker and writer," the longshoreman philosopher held. "To do otherwise would be to feel a pretentious fraud."[21]

The frequent labor stoppages, occasional dock injury, and set-your-own-hours schedule of his waterfront vocation proved congenial to his writing avocation. Though the fixed job site differed from his decade as a migrant worker, the loose docket on the docks resembled his previous existence. "I average about 40 bucks a week which is more than enough to live on," Hoffer noted in 1949. "And all I have to do is put in 20 hours of actual work. It is a racket, and I love it."[22] A waterfront strike in 1946 allowed Hoffer the leisure to begin writing *The True Believer*. A waterfront strike in 1948 gave him the leisure to finish it.[23]

In the years surrounding *The True Believer*, Hoffer lodged in San Francisco's increasingly ghettoized Fillmore section. The blue-collar intellectual's room contained an uncomfortable chair, a phonograph, a radio, a writing board, a kitchenette used to make tea, a bookcase, and a bed that folded into a closet. More startling than what the spartan cell contained is what it didn't. "I could not find your name in the phone book," one baffled correspondent reported, while another explained to a perhaps bemused Hoffer that "you are a hard man to reach by telephone."[24] Until his last years in the 1980s, Eric Hoffer had neither television nor telephone. His closet contained no suit and tie, items foregone even when he visited the White House. He lived, always, alone. "He had to have his privacy," Lili Osborne recalled. "He had to lie down and go to sleep when he wanted to lie down and go to sleep—or get up at three in the morning."[25]

It was in this solitary environment, liberated from the influence of people and common electronic communications devices, that an American original penned originality to paper.

From 1438 McAllister Street, a bald, bespectacled, burly gentleman, puffing on a pipe, a cigar, or whatever tobacco-smoking instrument proved handy, could be spied venturing forth to the bus stop, where he would catch a ride to Golden Gate Park. "The best way for me to think is to be on the road, to walk," Hoffer maintained. "I've written *The True Believer* actually at the Golden Gate Park, starting from 8th Avenue. . . . By the time I come to the beach I have black and white."[26] The pedestrian and chauffeured—even if on a crowded city bus—existence facilitated a life of the mind.

A notebook, usually one that could fit snugly into a coat pocket, accompanied Hoffer on his San Francisco strolls. His aphoristic writing took shape therein. Amidst a doodle of a skeleton wearing a turban, lists of books to buy, and a weekly budget showing $34 in necessities out of $48.20 in pay, the notebooks offered punchy treasures, such as: "The more zeal, the less heart. To put one's heart into something often results in heartlessness."[27] The best material from the notebooks Hoffer transferred onto note cards. The best of the cards made their way back into the notebooks, in which he wrote his books in quite legible longhand. "The important part of his writing was going over it and rewriting and rewriting," Osborne remembered. "That to him was a joy—to take the work, figuring out what to cut."[28]

The process resulted in writing that got straight to the point. Efficient and crisp, Hoffer's words stood out against the opaque, verbose, circuitous style that increasingly characterized the prose of intellectuals. If readers found his style original it was because they had never come across the French writers—Pascal, Montaigne, Renan, de la Rochefoucauld—whom he imitated. He had a habit of making big points in short sentences. He did so in part by deliberately exaggerating the point. Sightings of qualifiers—"perhaps," "seems," "on the other hand," "for the most part"—are scarce. The straightforward sentences catalyze thinking. They have a why-didn't-I-think-of-that quality, exemplifying Hoffer's definition of a philosopher as one who tells you what is right under your nose.[29] The sharp writing coldcocked many a reader into epiphany:

- "There is always a chance that he who sets himself up as his brother's keeper will end up by being his jailkeeper."[30]
- "Nothing is so unsettling to a social order as the presence of a mass of scribes without suitable employment and an acknowledged status."[31]
- "We are discovering that broken habits can be more painful and crippling than broken bones, and that disintegrating values may have as deadly a fallout as disintegrating atoms."[32]
- "One of the surprising privileges of intellectuals is that they are free to be scandalously asinine without harming their reputation."[33]
- "Rudeness is the weak man's imitation of strength."[34]
- "What starts out here as a mass movement ends up as a racket, a cult, or a corporation."[35]

Short sentences begat short paragraphs begat short books, many of which are not so much proper books, like

The True Believer, as they are collections of essays, maxims culled from notebooks, and printed diary entries. Characteristically, not one of Hoffer's books eclipses two hundred pages, and he legated a prize for essays that do not exceed five hundred words—enough for two-and-a-half original ideas by his count.[36]

Averse to typewriters, Hoffer hired strangers off the street to type his manuscripts.[37] "And now a difficult subject: I send you a longhand copy," Hoffer wrote in a draft letter to Margaret Anderson. "The thing ought to be typed by a literate person, someone who understands more or less what he copies and who can correct a misspelled word or some particularly monstrous turn of phrase. It would take me weeks to find such a person here."[38] Ultimately, the "literate person" typing the *True Believer* manuscript turned out to be Anderson, paid a hundred dollars for the task.[39]

The typescript went off to Harper & Brothers in New York. Perhaps seeing himself in its pages, Evan Thomas found *The True Believer* "an extremely cynical work." The member of the first family of American socialism advised Harper & Brothers to reject the book. John Fischer criticized Hoffer's penchant for broad generalization and lack of illustrations to bolster the point. Nevertheless, he judged *The True Believer* "an important piece of original thinking," adding, "I very much hope we can work out a contract to publish it."[40] Harper did. "The only moment of unalloyed happiness I ever had was when I received a wire from Harper telling me that they would publish *The True Believer*," Hoffer remembered. "I felt like a darling of fate, an immortal raised above the common run of humanity."[41]

The True Believer

The 1951 book bequeaths a name to "the man of fanatical faith who is ready to sacrifice his life for a holy cause."[42] That "holy cause" need not be religious, and usually isn't. Any cause will do for the true believer. The personality attracted to Communism might also be ready for Nazism, fascism, Christianity, Islam, Zionism, or whatever movement comes along. He longs to belong.

The true believer is the activist impenetrable to reason; the celebrity joiner indiscriminately affixing his name to diverse petitions; the placard-waving protester repeating the lie until belief; the excited ideologue whose a priori wisdom overrides the facts before him. People who have never read Hoffer demonstrate his impact by their frequent use of the phrase "true believer" within political parlance. Thus, a religious phrase became, primarily, a political one.

Mass movements act as the religion for people who reject religion. The cause to which true believers dedicate themselves invariably contains the trappings of the superstitions they rail against—holy books, ceremonies, sacrifice, excommunication, professions of faith, high priests, saints, etc. The ideologies of the twentieth century created a vacuum and then filled it. "For though ours is a godless age," Hoffer wrote, "it is the very opposite of irreligious."[43]

"Mass movements can rise and spread without belief in a God," Hoffer wrote, "but never without belief in a devil."[44] More important to Nazism than Hitler was the Jew; more important to Communism than Stalin was the capitalist. Hatred unifies the mass movement in a way that love cannot.

The mass movement is a mob. It is thus susceptible to all the viciousness that a mob mentality engenders. Compounding the dangers of mob psychology is the psychological state of those attracted to the mob. It is the nature of mass movements to attract losers. The faith gained in the cause replaces the faith lost in oneself. The misfit, who blames society rather than himself for his misfortune, fits the cause that seeks to change society. The cause fits the misfit by providing a rationalization for his resentments. A meaningless existence, perhaps devoid of friends and social life, suddenly glows with meaning. The true believer is never alone. He has comrades, not friends. Their devotion to the cause creates an illusion of mutual loyalty that is shattered immediately upon one's separation from the cause. Threaten the cause—with an idea, with ridicule, with defection, with suppression—and the true believer will react as if you have threatened his life. This is because you have.

The cause provides the joiner with a line, relieving him of the burden to think. Propaganda serves the movement not by convincing the unconverted but by allowing the true believer to more easily lie to himself. The ideology provides the Rosetta Stone for understanding the past and the crystal ball for seeing the future. It offers a one-size-fits-all solution to life's mysteries. "To be in possession of an absolute truth is to have a net of familiarity spread over the whole of eternity. There are no surprises and no unknowns. All questions have already been answered, all decisions made, all eventualities foreseen."[45] Omniscience gives the true believer the confidence to act on his slogans. With convictions so right, what could be wrong (gas chambers, the gulag, death marches, beheadings) in their pursuit?

The cloistered nature of the movement shields the true believer from reality. Truth is whatever serves the movement; lies are whatever undermines it. *The True Believer* explains that "the effectiveness of a doctrine should not be judged by its profundity, sublimity or the validity of the truth it embodies, but by how thoroughly it insulates the individual from his self and the world as it is."[46]

The True Believer's reliance on great thinkers, aversion to contemporary anecdotes to buttress the point, and aphoristic style contributed to its timelessness. But the book was a reaction to the age of Hitler and Stalin. It rang true for so many readers because they had recently witnessed otherwise intelligent people delve into stupidity, otherwise good people commit acts of evil, otherwise independent people join the herd. *The True Believer* is one of the twentieth century's most important books because it helps us understand the twentieth century.

Friends in High Places

Hoffer's slim volume was enthusiastically received. Orville Prescott of the *New York Times*, who deemed the book one of the most important of the 1950s, wrote that *The True Believer* was "lumpy with challenging ideas," "a harsh and potent mental tonic" that "glitters with icy wit."[47] Philosopher Bertrand Russell praised the author's "almost uncanny psychological insight."[48] But neither the world's foremost public intellectual nor America's most influential book critic was Hoffer's most puissant advocate.

In the summer of 1951, an American general stationed in France passed on to a reporter a book that he had read. "It's about mass movements," the general explained. "The book analyzes why people turn to causes like Communism or Fascism."[49] About a year later, the American people elected the general their president. The book, Eric Hoffer's *True Believer*, skyrocketed in popularity because of its association with Dwight Eisenhower.

Look magazine dubbed Hoffer "Ike's Favorite Author," justifying the tag by noting that the president had recommended *The True Believer* to "so many of his friends that its author, Eric Hoffer, would seem to qualify as the President's favorite writer."[50] In 1956, the *New York Times* reported that the president was still urging *The True Believer* on friends.[51] Other officials in the Eisenhower administration caught the bug. *People Today* reported that "Defense Secretary [Charles Erwin] Wilson keeps a stack of copies behind his desk, to hand out to underlings and visitors."[52]

As late as 1959, Eisenhower continued to recommend *The True Believer*. "The mental stress and burden which this form of government imposes has been particularly well recognized in a little book about which I have spoken on several occasions," Eisenhower explained in a letter to a veteran from his World War II Army. "It is 'The True Believer,' by Eric Hoffer; you might find it of interest. In it, he points out that dictatorial systems make one contribution to their people which leads them to tend to support such systems—freedom from the necessity of informing themselves and making up their own minds concerning these tremendous[ly] complex and difficult questions."[53]

The president's reading habits, which betrayed a fondness for cowboy novels, had been ridiculed by intellectuals.[54] The man labeled his favorite author returned the contempt the intellectuals had heaped on the president.

"My knowledge of the intellectual is not based on firsthand experience," Hoffer conceded. "I've probably met half a dozen intellectuals all my life. I don't know them. But I always say to myself, 'If Marx, who never knew anything about the workingmen, who never done a day's work in his life, could write about workingmen, then why the heck shouldn't I be able to write about the intellectuals?'"[55]

Family Life for the Solitary Man

Shortly before the publication of *The True Believer*, Selden Osborne, an intellectual playing a workingman, invited fellow stevedore Hoffer, a workingman playing an intellectual, to dinner. Hoffer came back for seconds, and returned for more helpings every few days for the next thirty years. The solitary transient found in Osborne's family a surrogate family. "He became part of two families: a worker family and my family," recalled Lili Osborne, Selden's wife.[56] The visitor initially played a grandfatherly role among the Osbornes, prophesying correctly that the pregnant Lili would bear a boy and name him "Eric." Perhaps dissatisfied with his peripheral position, Hoffer gradually occupied a more central role in his friend Selden's household.

Hoffer developed a special relationship with Lili and her youngest son, Eric. Like all children, Eric Hoffer didn't entirely get other children. One gleans from his published diary, *Working and Thinking on the Waterfront*, that he mistook willfulness, lack of discipline, and moodiness as characteristics specific to this three-year-old rather than the universal condition of all three-year-olds. The big boy's moods toward the little boy oscillated as wildly as the little boy's moods toward the big boy. As glaring as Big Eric's bewilderment regarding Little Eric was his intense attachment. Hoffer regarded the child as the only person he had known since birth, and felt that they were in some way grafted together.[57]

Once a week, Hoffer would take his namesake and Lili to Fisherman's Wharf, Golden Gate Park, Mount Diablo, or some other Bay Area attraction.[58] As the little boy grew older, movies, particularly Westerns, became favorite pastimes. Hoffer bragged of seeing *Escape from Fort Bravo* a dozen times with young Eric, vowing to see it a thirteenth time should it be shown again.[59] Generous with money as well as time, Hoffer lavished stuffed animals, comic books, and clothes upon the boy. He even paid nursery school tuition. Hoffer's bare-bones needs— tobacco, books, food, rent, clothes, bus fare—required little of his earnings. So he set up a trust fund for young Eric.[60] Selden enjoyed Hoffer's freehandedness as Hoffer enjoyed his friendship—even as Hoffer's friendship with Selden's wife deepened.[61]

Hoffer's published journal entries on the Osbornes read like an anthropologist's observations among a newly discovered tribe. Living a largely fly-by-night and wholly anonymous existence since leaving New York, the fiftysomething bachelor wasn't habituated to socializing within a family unit. "A stay in the Osborne house usually depresses me," Hoffer noted. "Yet I love every one of them. In my attitude toward them there is a mixture of warm compassion and irksome annoyance. At some moments I am convinced that I am being drained and bled. I also have now and then a sense of approaching doom. With Selden's somber sulking, Tonia's epilepsy,

Lili's spells of thoughtlessness, anything may happen."[62] If it dawned on Hoffer that he may have been a source of the chaos he described, he never put it down on paper.

An oversized body with an oversized personality regularly held court at the Osbornes' dinner table. The introduction of a boisterous de facto family member coincided with the disintegration of Lili and Selden's marriage, the unwelcome publicity of Osborne family matters in Hoffer's works, and the sudden death of daughter Tonia. The loud and opinionated longshoreman left rough seas in his wake. Feeling betrayed by his inclusion in a volume of published diaries that Hoffer had indicated he would leave unpublished, Little Eric unloaded on Big Eric. He accused him of multiple deceits, and implored the author to leave him out of future books. "I remember your constant ugly arguments with Tonia," a grown-up Little Eric explained to Big Eric. "If you'd been more humane, and let it be, I felt then, she'd have struggled through and might still be around today."[63]

In dark moments, Hoffer may have looked upon such turbulence as vindicating his reluctance to connect deeply with other human beings. But he undoubtedly learned that putting his heart out there risked not only getting it broken but having it filled as well. The reward was apparently worth the risk. Hoffer remained a part of the Osborne family for the remainder of his life, gave and received love, and bequeathed the copyright of his works to Lili.

"A One-Man Happening"

By the 1960s, a reviewer observed that "California's guru" was "a man who is becoming something of a legend," while a writer in the *Wall Street Journal* deemed Hoffer "a phenomenon, a one-man happening."[64] A person who didn't watch television became a television star. Hearing Big Eric referenced on NBC News left an astonished Little Eric to exclaim, "Mother! He's talking about Baba!"[65] Reintroduced to egghead America in the mid-1960s through a series of interviews on National Educational Television, Hoffer exploded into mainstream America's living rooms in late 1967 in the first of two prime-time specials on CBS. The network dubbed the response, which ultimately included an Emmy Award, "unprecedented."[66] Television crews erupted in cheers upon its completion.[67] Interviewer Eric Sevareid told of a flood of letters and telegrams inundating the network: "The switchboard at virtually every CBS station carrying the broadcast had lit up like a Christmas tree."[68] Viewers dubbed Hoffer "a modern Elijah" and "a current Socrates."[69] Reflecting the personal connection many felt with Hoffer through the airwaves, one well-wisher simply wrote: "I wish I could get 'pee eyed' with you some evening."[70]

The most ecstatic viewer resided at 1600 Pennsylvania Avenue. Days after the 1967 broadcast, Eric Hoffer and Lyndon Johnson toasted Frescas under a magnolia tree on the South Lawn of the White House. The former West Texas schoolteacher and the recently retired San Francisco longshoreman hit it off like brothers from different mothers. Despite the eighty-degree temperature, Hoffer played his part by donning the obligatory flannel jacket and work boots. He apologized to Johnson for not accepting a previous invitation to a state dinner because it required a tie—a fashion appendage Hoffer refused to wear. The president responded that a tieless Hoffer should just show up next time and Johnson would remove his tie in solidarity. A scheduled five minutes turned into fifty. Johnson's White House invitation validated Hoffer in a manner akin to Eisenhower's unsolicited promotion. Hoffer's nationally televised appraisal of the president as the century's greatest validated Johnson at a time when even the house intellectuals in his employ sniffed behind his back.[71]

Whereas 1951's *True Believer* was characterized by the author's steely detachment, the Hoffer of the 1960s was a combatant, rather than a removed observer, in the culture wars. "Which side are you on?" went a familiar query of the era. Eric Hoffer chose the side of the squares. On every major question, he stood forcefully against the zeitgeist. In the process, a Middle American hero was reborn.

He did this from the heart of the counterculture. In 1964, thanks in part to Selden Osborne's prodding of college-roommate-turned-Berkeley-chancellor Clark Kerr, the political science department at the University of California's flagship campus hired Hoffer to hold weekly bull sessions with students. During the 1930s, Hoffer had bused the dirty dishes of students and professors at an all-night Berkeley eatery. Now, three decades later, the dishwasher held office hours in Barrows Hall from 2 P.M. to 5 P.M. every Wednesday. Arriving at Berkeley shortly before the Free Speech Movement's demands, building takeovers, and vandalism set the template for campus activism, Hoffer necessarily clashed with students. "'Don't trust anyone over thirty'—now, what the hell does that mean?" Hoffer asked *The New Yorker*'s Calvin Tomkins. "To me, they haven't raised a blade of grass, they haven't laid a brick, they don't know a goddamned thing, and here they sit in judgment! Besides which, you know, they talk an awful lot of crap. I just don't see why we should go down on our knees and accept this nonsense and clap hands. What is to be gained by humoring them?"[72]

Observing the temper tantrums of pampered youth firsthand, Hoffer expanded upon ideas he had written extensively about in *The True Believer* and *The Ordeal of Change*. Just as change meant chaos and upheaval in a nation, a nation disproportionately comprised of people undergoing the chaos and upheaval inherent in youth's transition to adulthood necessarily meant national chaos and upheaval. "The presence of a global population of juveniles spells trouble for everybody," Hoffer explained in the *Saturday Review* in 1966. "No country is a good country for its juveniles, and even in normal times every society is in the grip of a crisis when a new generation passes from childhood to manhood. The enemy is within the gates."[73] The baby boom was no boom for civilization.

Appointed by Johnson to a presidential committee on violence in the wake of political assassinations, campus shutdowns, bombings, urban riots, and rising crime, Hoffer had explosive confrontations with witnesses and even a fellow committee member. In October 1968, he called student rioters "hoodlums," announced that he refused to take a student radical witness seriously even if his fellow commission members did, buried his face in his hands as another radical leader, Tom Hayden, testified, and walked out during the former SDS president's remarks. Later that week, he engaged in a shouting match with a witness justifying urban violence; fellow committeeman Leon Higginbotham responded by denouncing Hoffer as embracing the "racist philosophy of this country."[74] The blowup between the San Francisco longshoreman and the federal judge, both appointed by the same president, demonstrated the inevitability of the Democratic Party's disintegration then under way.

Hoffer at his worst made headlines by calling for a violent crackdown on student violence. "It would have been a wonderful thing," a table-pounding Hoffer testified before a Senate committee, "if [Columbia president] Grayson Kirk got mad and got a gun and killed a few" of those who had taken over the Ivy League campus in the spring of 1968.[75]

Hoffer loved America and many of his adversaries professed not to. This explains the mutual venom. So, too, does the clash of cultures. Hoffer represented America's possibilities. He made something out of nothing. The rich-kid activists and privileged intellectuals embodied decadent ingratitude spawned by America's bounty. Hoffer's patriotism stemmed from the belief that America was the workingman's country. That the everyman became president hardly proved America's mediocrity; it proved the excellence of the American everyman. Hoffer admired the mundane manner in which his countrymen achieved the momentous. National greatness didn't come from a wise man's design. It came organically from ordinary blokes. That, he figured, accounted for much of the resentment from intellectuals, who lacked importance in such an egalitarian society.[76] Merely to highlight America's qualities during this cynical era invited conflict.

Hoffer's support of the Vietnam War, and kind words for the men who oversaw that war—Presidents Johnson and Nixon—set him apart from intellectuals of the era. "Sen. Ribicoff displayed historical illiteracy when he accused Mayor Daley and the Chicago police of being Gestapo," Hoffer reflected about 1968's violent peace protests outside of the Democratic National Convention. "It was precisely because the Weimer Republic had no Daleys and no Chicago police to fight its battles in Germany's cities during the 1920s that the Nazis and their Gestapo came to power."[77]

Hoffer shared much in common with his youthful adversaries. He had lived as a premature hippie on LA's skid row in the 1920s and as a nomadic worker in the 1930s. In San Francisco, he resided among the hippies. "If it wasn't for the question of drugs," he noted, "I would be all for the hippies because it's a healthy reaction against the rat race."[78] But San Francisco was changing too quickly for his liking. He repeatedly complained of the increasing difficulty of identifying the sex of people he passed on the street.[79] He wrote, "In the San Francisco Bay area you see the young beset and preyed upon by vultures, wolves and parasites: dope peddlers, pimps, lechers, perverts, thugs, cult mongers, and ideological seducers. Everywhere you look you can see human beings rot before they ripen."[80] The world was becoming a different place, and nowhere was it as strange as San Francisco. "Many times, I step out of my room, I go down to Polk Street, I feel like an immigrant who just arrived in a foreign country," Hoffer explained on CBS. "And it's a helluva job to immigrate at sixty-seven."[81]

On the waterfront, on campus, and on the bum, Hoffer had always lived as the stranger in a strange land. African Americans peopled the apartments surrounding the McAllister Street flat in which he resided for most of the 1940s and '50s, and the succeeding Clay Street address sat firmly within Chinatown. On the docks, Hoffer worked alongside a disproportionate number of blacks. Despite decades living and working alongside people of color, he elicited cries of racism for his harsh assessment of the civil-rights movement and its pale-faced camp followers. Among the latter group were his New York editors, who unsuccessfully lobbied him to tone down his words—even to the point of asking him to bowdlerize sections of his private journals upon publication.[82]

"If you think that the Negro is your equal, then you expect something from him," Hoffer bluntly informed a prime-time CBS audience. "On the other hand, if you think that the Negro is your inferior, that he is incapable of doing anything, then you want to treat him with extra special care, and you want to make him more equal than equal."[83] Hoffer's views on race were complex and, characteristically, original. He deemed racism so pervasive that if a black Jesus Christ were to appear, white America would see black first and Jesus second. Yet he castigated African Americans for relying on external beneficence to boost group pride. He believed that they must collectively contribute something of worth to society to feel pride.[84] "Fuzzy wuzzy hairdos, animal teeth necklaces, and Swahili patter cannot produce one atom of genuine pride."[85] He never adequately explained how an individual affected the type of collective contribution to the world that he believed would instill group pride. Though his promotion of self-sufficiency echoed the message of the Black Panthers, then ascendant in the Bay Area, he ridiculed the group's leaders. "Phony. Phony," Hoffer said of Eldridge Cleaver on national television. "Look at that misbegotten Cleaver—a sewer rat if ever there was one. Talking about *Soul on Ice*—it's 'soul on manure' if you ask me."[86]

In the *Star Wars* bar scene that was the Bay Area in the 1960s, Eric Hoffer played the most exotic alien of all. Amidst militaristic Black Panthers, drugged-out flower children, flamboyant homosexuals, vacant-eyed cultists, leather-clad Hell's Angels, and strident student radicals, the burly senior citizen clad in 1940s workman's clothes with closely cropped white hair bordering a bald dome elicited stares. Hoffer was the other side of the '60s, the protohardhat, one-man not-so-silent majority, Archie Bunker intellectual who loudly rebutted the trendy nostrums of the times. In a popular newspaper column, articles for *Harper's*, *Playboy*, and *Saturday Review*, and books such as *The Temper of Our Time* and *The Ordeal of Change*, Eric Hoffer put his finger on the '60s in real time. Here, Hoffer speaks heresies to the epoch from his position in the heart of the counterculture; there, CBS pays Hoffer for the privilege of featuring him in prime-time specials in which he mocks Eugene McCarthy, Ronald Reagan, Arthur Schlesinger, and John F. Kennedy.[87] The decade saw Hoffer quoted in a presidential speech, deliver an inaugural oration for San Francisco mayor Joseph Alioto, and engage Berkeley radicals on their home turf. To paraphrase the Beatles, Eric Hoffer was here, there, and everywhere in the 1960s.

As the 1960s yielded to the 1970s, the Stevedore Socrates yielded to other spokesmen incapable of filling his work boots. "I should sit in my corner and not say anything," an exhausted Hoffer explained upon giving up his $5,000-a-week column appearing in four hundred or so papers. "I'm not convinced any more that I know the score."[88]

Old age, emphysema, and ailments stemming from a workingman's life sidetracked him in his final years. Along with the shore and his column, he retired from the Berkeley position as well. He emerged from semi-retirement to appear on *Dinah Shore* and in the pages of *People*, and he wrote half of his life's books in these golden years. But he kept a lower profile than he had during the hectic previous decade. The scourges that he had warned against during the '60s took no such sabbatical. The San Francisco hangover—Altamont, the Zebra killings, the Symbionese Liberation Army, Jonestown, etc.—ensured that a prophet without honor in his own house got a begrudging second look from '60s skeptics.

In May 1983, a month after being awarded the Presidential Medal of Freedom by a politician he had once dismissed as a "B" actor trying to turn California into a "B" movie, Hoffer died at the age of eighty.[89] Or was it eighty-four?

Better Than Fiction, Not Quite Fact

"It all depends how a story ends," our protagonist once explained, "not how a story begins."[90] He could have been speaking of his own life. We don't know how the Eric Hoffer story began. We know only that in the last half of his life he emerged from obscurity to provide some of the most insightful observations about human behavior. The verifiable Eric Hoffer is more captivating than the mythic one. Life trumped art.

In an age of calcifying ideologies, the union Democrat was hard to pigeonhole. He was an independent thinker because he was independent of influence beyond his experience, study, and observation. No think tank, little magazine, or political party owned his opinion. His ideas stood alone because he did. The free agent's originality stemmed from his time away from people and the devices they use to communicate. By being unplugged, the urban monk made people want to plug into him.

Swimming against the current helps explain his popularity. So do the key ways in which he conformed to trends. It was an era of efficiency. If factory lines and offices benefited from streamlining, so did prose. His crisp writing seems as well suited to the era of '60s automation as it does to the world of blogs, Twitter, and six-second sound bites. For Hoffer, big books obscured what the author didn't know while slim ones offered no hiding places.[91] His aphorisms, columns, and books were open to all without reducing all to the lowest common denominator. Accessible need not mean dumb.

A critic who wondered, "I don't know if we have elevated him out of a romantic, mythic need to discover a new Thoreau," was on to something.[92] As the idiot box encouraged image-conscious activists and public intellectuals, the hulking senior citizen busting out of his dockworker's garb stood out as the most colorful cartoon character. Consciously or unconsciously, the longshoreman philosopher played a part that audiences could not get enough of. His intellectual rags-to-riches story—from blindness to bibliophile, from skid row to the White House, from the docks to the best-seller list—undoubtedly helped create the mystique.

"So in retrospect those twenty years are a procession of stories in which truth and fiction are so interwoven that I cannot tell them apart," Hoffer wrote of days living on skid row and the rails in his appropriately titled memoir *Truth Imagined*. "I might almost say that I remember most minutely and distinctly things that did not happen to me."[93] Part of the fun of Eric Hoffer is what we know. Most of the fun is that we don't know much.

5

Poet of the Pulps

How a Down-and-Out Outcast Wrote
His Way into the In-Crowd

"Atelephone makes man a monkey on a string,"
explained the phone-phobic Eric Hoffer. "The
phone rings and you are completely hooked until the
other person wants to let you go. Then you are free
until the next ring."[1] Hoffer sounded eerily like Albert
Brock, a character in Ray Bradbury's short story "The
Murderer." "The telephone's such a *convenient* thing; it
just sits there and *demands* you call someone who doesn't
want to be called. Friends were always calling, calling,
calling me," lamented Brock.[2] Eric Hoffer had much in
common with Ray Bradbury, a teller of the future who
lived as though in the distant past, a Left Coast denizen
whose writings paid homage to Middle America, and an
intellectual standing athwart the political correctness of
intellectual poseurs.

Born in Waukegan, Illinois, on August 22, 1920,
Bradbury insists he remembers the day vividly.[3] Evi-
dences of the poverty of the family he was born into

were many. When the influenza epidemic of 1918 took one of Bradbury's older brothers, the family had not the money for a burial marker. The living room moonlighted as a bedroom, where Ray and brother Skip shared a pullout sofa. The bed-sharing accommodations lasted until Ray's marriage. In 1938, Ray graduated from high school wearing his only suit, which his uncle had been wearing when murdered by a stick-up man six years earlier. It still sported the bullet hole.[4] Losing his job as a lineman for the power and light company, the family patriarch led several failed ventures west before finding permanent work in Los Angeles when Ray was thirteen.

If Ray's poverty didn't stand out during an impoverished age, his awkward nature did. "Ray was a rather boisterous young boy," remembered Forrest Ackerman, the coiner of the phrase "sci-fi" who knew Bradbury as a teenager. "He liked to imitate Hitler and W. C. Fields. It's a wonder we didn't strangle him."[5] While other kids played sports, sickly Ray read. "When I was a kid I was mad for *Prince Valiant* and *Tarzan*; they were two of my favorites and I collected them for years," he remembers. "I loved Edgar Rice Burroughs. In fact one of the first stories I ever wrote was a sequel to one of the *John Carter of Mars* stories. I also loved Poe's *Tales of Mystery and Imagination*, which my aunt, Neva, gave to me when I was about twelve. I loved reading those stories over and over again."[6] Like the old man in "To the Chicago Abyss," the young man who would later write that story was "a trash heap of the mediocre."[7]

With roller skates on his feet and zits on his face, the teenaged Bradbury, like so many of his future readers, was a nerd's nerd. He lost his virginity only by paying a fleshy redheaded prostitute.[8] Even the local science-fiction group eschewed his company, encouraging him, according to his biographer, to "sit off to the side and drink Coca-Colas as the rest of the group sipped alcoholic beverages."[9]

The reject dared to plot the ultimate acceptance: stardom. During his brief stay in Tucson, thirteen-year-old Ray played hanger-on to the workers at KGAR until they permitted him to read Sunday comics on the air and provide sound effects for the in-studio programs. In Los Angeles, he relentlessly pursued autographs outside of studio gates, bagging the signatures of W. C. Fields, Judy Garland, and Marlene Dietrich. Hoping to get George Murphy's attention, he hung upside down from a tree like a monkey outside the actor's home. He dumpster-dived for discarded scripts of the *Hollywood Hotel* radio show outside the Figueroa Street Playhouse. George Burns flattered the tenth grader by praising the amateurish scripts he had given him. Burns and Gracie Allen even concluded a 1936 broadcast by using a joke that Bradbury had pushed on them.[10] These acts of kindness and recognition undoubtedly inspired the child writer to dream big dreams.

When he realized those dreams, Bradbury was quick to let everybody know. After Arkham House published Ray's first book, *Dark Carnival*, in 1947, he returned to the corner where he had sold the Los Angeles *Herald Express*, tracking down old customers and displaying the bound proof of his success. Years later, this childlike tendency reared its amusing head when the author enthusiastically purchased seventy tickets for his friends, family, and tangential acquaintances for the premiere of *Moby Dick*, the John Huston film whose script Bradbury had penned.[11]

He was proud *and* protective of his work. Huston's expropriation of cowriter credit sent Bradbury complaining to the screenwriters guild, where he ultimately lost his case, then to his desk, where the pen proved mightier than intraguild litigation, to write "Banshee," which depicts Huston as a mean-spirited, bullying cad.[12] In 1961, Bradbury successfully sued CBS and *Playhouse 90* for purloining *Fahrenheit 451* for an episode of the program.[13] He famously accused Rod Serling of *The Twilight Zone* of cribbing his oeuvre.[14] Even gotcha documentarian Michael Moore felt Bradbury's wrath when he borrowed the name *Fahrenheit 451*, certainly common cultural property by this point, for his anti–George W. Bush *Fahrenheit 9/11* movie. Bradbury, who made a career of borrowing from other writers to title his own works—"Something Wicked This Way Comes" (Shakespeare), "Usher II" (Poe), "The Golden Apples of the Sun" (Yeats), "Here There Be Tygers" (Benét), etc.—called Moore an "asshole" and accused him of stealing.[15] However tempting it might be to blame these *Fahrenheit 9/11* grievances on politics (Bradbury has been a stalwart Republican for decades[16]), the writer's pattern of mistaking homage for plagiarism (save when *he* paid homage) best explains the kerfuffle.

Inside the man who wrote such pop-culture masterpieces as *Fahrenheit 451* and *The Martian Chronicles* was the insecure mama's boy rejected by girls, beaten up by boys, and cast out by the outcasts. He had made his success the hard way, and he wasn't going to allow freeloaders to come along for the ride.

The Outsider

In the one field where the fledgling writer should have felt welcome, he remained the outsider. A blue-collar midwestern background made him an alien species to the literati. In form, venue, and genre, Bradbury's writings widened the gap between the Middle American nerd and his coastal critics.

It is telling that he expressed himself in one of the most democratic of all literary forms: the short story. Whereas many critics wish to attend a more exclusive party, everyone is invited to the short story. Its accessibility, efficiency, and immediate payoff made it the literary medium fit to compete in an age of mass communications. If Bradbury didn't have the patience to write a novel, he benefited from the decreasing attention spans of Americans who didn't have the patience to read them. Even Bradbury's "novels" are often elongated short stories (*Fahrenheit 451*, *Something Wicked This Way Comes*) or collections of short stories (*The Martian Chronicles*, *Dandelion Wine*) disguised as novels. In the latter case, the imposition of a loose, unifying narrative on otherwise unconnected chapters generally created the illusion of continuity from a series of stand-alone stories.

If all-too-accessible short stories didn't do enough to offend highbrows, the venues where Bradbury's work appeared cemented his reputation as a crowd-pleaser estranged from critics. Before being bound between paper covers for mass-market editions, Bradbury's stories appeared in the pulps and even in an emerging girlie magazine. *Playboy* serialized *Fahrenheit 451* in its early numbers. Other destinations for his writings included *Dime Detective*, *Weird Tales*, and *Amazing Stories*.

After appearing in the pulps, Bradbury's stories reached a mass audience through radio serials and television anthology series. In 1946, Bradbury sold his first story to radio, "Killer, Come Back to Me," a mediocre gangster narrative boasting a femme fatale and obligatory shootout with the FBI that aired on NBC's *Molle Mystery Theater* on May 17 of that year.[17] Bradbury's second radio story, "The Meadow," aired on ABC in early 1947 after its author won a contest.[18] Neither too proud to reject the patronage of "the heavier brushless shaving cream for tender skins" nor too humble to submit his work to a panel of judges, the fledgling was determined to win an audience. Bradbury discovered that sometimes winning an audience meant losing the critics.

The West Coast residency that proved disadvantageous to his publishing career worked in his favor for selling story rights to radio and television. Living in Los Angeles enabled him to cultivate relationships with network producers, such as AM heavyweights William Spier and Norman Corwin. In the waning days of radio's golden age, the young author placed nine stories on *Suspense*, ten stories on the pioneering sci-fi series *Dimension X* (amid works by Robert Heinlein, Isaac Asimov, and L. Ron Hubbard), eight on its revival *X Minus One*, and three on *Escape*. A story appearing on one show was no impediment to its appearance on another. For instance, "Zero Hour," a cautionary tale about lax parenting, appeared on *Suspense*, *Escape*, and *Lights Out*, while "Mars Is Heaven" got recycled by *Dimension X*, *Escape*, *Think: The ABC Radio Workshop*, and *X Minus One*.

While Bradbury reaped a minor financial windfall, he did not have control of his stories once sold to the networks. On the *X Minus One* treatment of "The

Veldt," for instance, the parents who allow their virtual-reality nursery to raise their children escape their brutal short-story fate as lunch to a pride of lions.[19] "The Crowd" of *Suspense*'s scriptwriters gawks not at the gory aftermath of car crashes but at the corpses left by a serial murderer.[20] *The Twilight Zone*'s revision of "I Sing the Body Electric," Bradbury's sole teleplay to air on the classic sci-fi program, left a particularly bitter taste. "They cut out the most important part of the story," Bradbury lamented. "The moment of truth in the story when the grandmother tells them that she is a robot."[21] Habitually revising his already published works, the author did not look kindly on meddlers who did the same. Alfred Hitchcock's fidelity to the text on episodes of his television series based on Bradbury stories intensified the author's admiration for the director.[22] When the television program bearing the sci-fi scribe's name aired between 1985 and 1992, *The Ray Bradbury Theater* significantly didn't just rely exclusively on his stories; it employed him as sole scriptwriter. Alas, "Even with *Ray Bradbury Theater* things had to be cut or shortened to accommodate the format," he recalls, resigned, in his nineties, to the inevitability of outside alterations.[23]

Bradbury's forays into radio, television, film, and even theater expanded his readership; it didn't impress critics. His work inhabited the lowbrow section of the newsstand, and moving out of that intellectual ghetto would take three attributes Ray Bradbury possessed in abundance: imagination, hard work, and persistence.

By penning tales of Martians and supernatural carnivals and robots, Bradbury had pigeonholed himself in the unfashionable category of science fiction. The prevailing attitude regarding the emerging genre was that it was kids' stuff. The bards of sci-fi ranked somewhere above comic book scribes and below spy novelists. But as Bradbury argued, George Orwell and Aldous Huxley wrote science fiction without wearing the label as a hair shirt. Why must he?[24] Bradbury wrote all kinds of fiction—detective stories, weird tales, gothic horror, etc.—outside of science fiction. But to some critics, he would always be a science-fiction writer, with all the limitations that the tag implies.

To science-fiction aficionados, though, Bradbury wasn't a science-fiction writer at all. His science fiction ignored sound science and concentrated on good fiction. "*Science Fiction Studies*, the most aggressively theoretical journal in the field, has never published a major article on Bradbury," report the authors of *Ray Bradbury: The Life of Fiction*. "Usually, he is mentioned as a point of comparison with other 'real' science fiction writers who are perceived as having the right stuff."[25] The feeling was mutual. Desperately seeking to escape the pigeonhole, Bradbury repeatedly sought to erase the pulp origins of his short stories by removing copyright references when the stories reappeared in his books.[26] He demanded that Doubleday delete the "science fiction" emblem that identified the genre to friendly readers but essentially told reviewers to ignore the book.[27]

Bradbury's hypersensitivity to the snob's sneer made him appear as the sneering snob to hard-core science-fiction geeks. He ran from them toward respectability. In a jailbreak from his pulp prison, Bradbury submitted short stories under the name "William Elliott" to mainline slicks *Mademoiselle*, *Charm*, and *Collier's*. All accepted within the same week in August 1945 and sent "Mr. Elliott" a total of a thousand dollars. Bradbury quickly informed the editors that checks should be redrafted, and bylines rewritten, giving him rather than his pen name credit.[28] He soon landed stories in *Harper's*, *The New Yorker*, and *Esquire*, won acceptance four times in the *Best American Short Stories* anthology, and earned a place in the O. Henry Prize Stories.

Everything about the midwestern transplant was uncouth, save his talent, which eventually even cool people could not deny. Ray Bradbury was happening in a hurry.

Bradbury and the Cognoscenti

It wasn't just the short-story accessibility, the sci-fi stigma, and the *Time*-magazine-bestowed "poet of the pulps" moniker that alienated insiders.[29] The content of the stories did, too.

His aesthetic sensibilities generally offended those who sat in judgment. When he flattered their political attitudes, or allowed them to project their ideology on his stories, the critics found a genius in the pulp fictioneer. Bradbury's only story ever accepted by *The New Yorker* is "I See You Never," an undeveloped fragment about the deportation of a Mexican illegal alien.[30] "I probably submitted over three or four hundred short stories to them over the years and this is the only one that ever sold," he recalls of the mediocre offering.[31] "I See You Never" was also one of the four Bradbury tales chosen for *Best American Short Stories*. Others selected were "The Big Black and White Game," which chronicles an interracial baseball game in which sore-loser whites quit, and "The Other Foot," which explores an African-

American-populated Mars considering imposing Jim Crow laws on white settlers fleeing an Earth ravaged by nuclear war.[32] Among the four honored, only "The Day It Rained Forever" carried an apolitical theme.[33] It was almost as if the bard of tattooed carnies, Martian ghost towns, and endless summer vacations merited recognition only for the tiny fraction of his catalog easily lending itself to politicization.

"His three short plays, under the general title The World of Ray Bradbury, ran for nearly a year in Los Angeles—but closed after a few days in Manhattan," observed admirer Russell Kirk. "The rising generation in Los Angeles (of whom Bradbury is the chief hero) loved those three plays—*The Veldt*, *To the Chicago Abyss*, and *The Pedestrians* [*sic*]. Yet the New York play-reviewers were more ferocious with Ray Bradbury than with any other man of mark in my memory, and they succeeded promptly in preventing anyone in New York from perceiving those truths which are best revealed by fable and parable. The rising generation of Manhattan was left with such plays as *The Toilet* for ethical instruction."[34]

What attracted the cognoscenti tells us more about them than about Bradbury. What caused the critics to scatter called the crowd to gather.

Bradbury dared mouth heresies offending the cult of technology, the dominant faith of the age. He paid homage to the family and to small-town America when the pack of individualists demanded conformity in its attack upon the family and small-town America. And he stood athwart political correctness before such a term came into vogue.

"Nostalgic Visionary"

"Video games are a waste of time for men with nothing else to do," Bradbury explained to Salon.com in 2001. "Real brains don't do that. On occasion? Sure. As relaxation? Great. But not full time and a lot of people are doing that. And while they're doing that, I'll go ahead and write another novel." He expressed similar disdain for automated teller machines: "Why go to a machine when you can go to a human being?"[35] "The Internet is a big distraction," he told the *New York Times* in 2008. "It's meaningless; it's not real. It's in the air somewhere."[36] For anyone who had read Bradbury's fiction, the apostasy against the gods Google, Microsoft, and Xbox did not surprise.

In Bradbury's imagination, the primitive contraptions dreamt up in basement laboratories by quixotic amateur Edisons prove the most wondrous creations. In *Dandelion Wine*, Bradbury's dilettante scientist Leo Auffmann invents virtual reality through a "cogs and wheels" backyard contraption he calls the "Happiness Machine." Auffmann asks, "How have we used machines so far, to make people cry? Yes! Every time man and the machine look like they will get on all right—boom! Someone adds a cog, airplanes drop bombs on us, cars run us off cliffs."[37] The time machine that the midwestern boys stumble upon in *Dandelion Wine* is not of the Doctor Who variety, but is an old man who brings the youngsters back in time through storytelling.[38] The rocket in the story of the same name is scrap purchased by Fiorello Bodoni, a poor man who dreams a rich man's dream by taking his children on an illusory journey to Mars in a spaceship dormant in the junkyard.[39]

In glaring contrast to virtuous throwback technology is the nightmarish science of the distant future and all-too-close present, which unleashes unintended consequences, technological servants turning the tables on human masters, and scientific advances bringing humanity backward. The television is "an unholy ghost," an "electronic beast" that "bleached" the mind.[40] The automobile is "the greatest destroyer of souls in history."[41] Telephones are impersonal gadgets that divorced words from meanings and drained personality from people.[42] Progress wasn't.

The science-fiction writer's skepticism of science is perhaps best exemplified in the stories "Almost the End of the World," "The Murderer," and "The Veldt."

In "Almost the End of the World," two miners reemerge from months at work to find civilization askew. Sunspots have blown out all television and radio transmissions. To fill the void, former viewers paint their houses, can fruit, learn to play musical instruments, bowl, and hold keg parties. In place of watching life they live life. A barber tells the two miners of the onscreen-black-and-white-fuzz-inducing event, "It was like a good friend who talks to you in your front room and suddenly shuts up and lies there, pale, and you know he's dead and you begin to turn cold yourself." Without televised company, people are forced to converse with other people. The victims dub the event the "Great Oblivion," an ironic phrase that in Bradbury's mind clearly refers to life after television's birth rather than after its imagined death.[43]

The title character in "The Murderer" kills mobile phones, car radios, televisions, and other electronic devices. Obviously insane to his captors, Albert Brock tells his story of a one-man revolution against invasive communications to the prison psychiatrist, whose wrist radio he promptly bites to death. The Murderer explains his motivations for drowning his office's intercom in hot coffee. "In *touch*! *There's* a slimy phrase. Touch, hell. *Gripped*! Pawed, rather. Mauled and massaged and pounded by FM voices." He employs chocolate ice cream to assassinate his car's radio. "That car radio cackling all day, Brock go here, Brock go there, Brock check in, Brock check out, okay Brock, hour lunch, Brock, lunch over, Brock, Brock, Brock. Well, that silence was like putting ice cream in my ears." On the bus, he interferes with the transmission of the various electronic gizmos used by his fellow riders. "The bus inhabitants faced with having to converse with each other. Panic! Sheer, animal panic!" He kills his television with a pistol. That is when the state comes for him.[44] The Murderer is the sane man living in an insane world. That the insane world so closely resembles ours, and increasingly so sixty years after the story's appearance, makes for one of Bradbury's most prescient and provocative yarns.

In one of Bradbury's most popular tales, "The Veldt," technology tears asunder the parent-child relationship. The Hadleys' "Happylife Home" projects the imagination of children Peter and Wendy onto three-dimensional screens in the nursery. So captivating is the toy that parents George and Lydia become obsolete. Foreshadowing the generational conflict that would plague the succeeding decade, 1950's "The Veldt" depicts a "nothing's too good for our children" parental attitude that spoils children, who lecture their parents as if they were son and daughter and not father and mother. The decision to turn off their futuristic house comes too late, as Peter and Wendy wish their parents dead—a dream the African Veldt-like three-dimensional playroom is only too happy to fulfill.[45]

Bradbury's fiction foreshadowed his lifestyle. When his stories and teleplays ran on 1950s anthology series, his growing brood did not watch because the Bradburys kept television out of their home—at least until the whole lot's 1955 bout with the measles compelled submission to the idiot box.[46] Bradbury in large part lived the atavistic outlook reflected in his science fiction. In his early years as a writer, perhaps more indicative of financial straits than technophobia, the phoneless Bradbury communicated to editors via a telephone booth at a gas station across from his home. He plugged away at a typewriter, and never got the hang of a computer. "A computer is a typewriter," he explained. "I have two typewriters, I don't need another one."[47] Anyone who has read "The Crowd," an early weird story that draws on Bradbury's experience witnessing the aftermath of a deadly car crash, grasps why he never learned to drive.[48] In 1968, the Aviation-Space Writers awarded Bradbury its highest honor for a *Life* magazine article on the space program. Notified of the honor just days before its presentation, the L.A.-based author could not accept his award in person at Cape Canaveral. The honoree of the Aviation-Space Writers did not fly.[49] The bard of the space age preferred nineteenth-century living.

The anecdotes illustrate the contrast at the heart of Ray Bradbury, atavist writer of science fiction. "He wrote of the far future," biographer Sam Weller explains in *The Bradbury Chronicles*, "but did it with the machines of old, cog-and-gear ironclad throwbacks to Wells and Verne; he wrote of the far past with a pained longing, as if to tell us all that our future would only be well served if we looked to yesteryear. Indeed, he was a contradiction. Ray Bradbury was a nostalgic visionary. He predicted the past and remembered the future."[50]

Hometown Happiness

Ray Bradbury's lifetime literary homage to unlocked doors, roaming bands of unsupervised kids, know-name neighbors, and green infiniteness owes a debt to his departure from Waukegan, Illinois, in late childhood. The cellophaned Americana of Bradbury's 1920s youth proved such a contrast to its boomtown Los Angeles replacement that it provided the fledgling author with a stock of memories that fueled decades of writing. If familiarity bred contempt, distance cultivated an apotheosized heartland for the transplant Los Angelino.

Nowhere is this more obvious than in "Mars Is Heaven" (redubbed "The Third Expedition" in *The Martian Chronicles*). Heaven turns out to be small-town America. In the story, a native of Green Bluff, Illinois, discovers Green Bluff, Illinois, on Mars. A son of Grinnell, Iowa, sees Grinnell, Iowa.[51] The author's heaven isn't seventy-two comely virgins or a welcoming committee of the famous people he had always wished to meet. It is sipping lemonade on the front porch with his grandparents in a sleepy town's summertime twilight. That is as much of a Rorschach test as anything in his fiction. Some people spend their first eighteen years planning jailbreaks from their hometowns. Bradbury spent his adult life fantasizing about returning to his.

He explained about the process of writing *Dandelion Wine*, "I sat me down to breakfasts, lunches, and dinners with the long dead and much loved. For I was a boy who did indeed love his parents and grandparents and his brother, even when that brother 'ditched' him."[52] The generational conflict that erupted shortly after the publication of *Dandelion Wine* and *Something Wicked This Way Comes* is nowhere present therein. Instead, Bradbury depicts generational harmony, in which younger brothers tag along with older siblings, the soon-dead dispense wisdom to the young, and quixotic men seek to escape midlife crises through "Happiness Machines."

Trendiness demanded that Bradbury hate his family and his hometown. He loved both.

Fahrenheit 451

The Bradbury story most read, watched, and heard is *Fahrenheit 451*. The dystopian novel warns of the dangers of political correctness, mind-numbing technology, and the laziness that discourages humans from living a human existence. Despite the arresting imagery conveyed by a title referring to the temperature at which paper burns, the threat to the life of the mind comes not as much from people who burn books as from people who don't read them. It's not matchstick technology but television, tranquilizers, conformism, and other social sedatives that smother the intellect.

Bradbury describes a future when "firemen" set fires (to books!) instead of putting them out. Suicide, drug use, vicarious living through television, antiseptic indoor hermitages, and day-care parenting by proxy are among the ways the book's characters escape from life's rewards and responsibilities. *Fahrenheit 451* chronicles the transformation of Guy Montag from model fireman who takes pleasure in burning books to a subversive who takes pleasure in reading them. Montag is found out by his firemen peers and flees to a subculture outside of the illiterate matrix. There, every inhabitant becomes a book—memorizing the great literary works so that they are not lost for posterity.

"You must understand that our civilization is so vast that we can't have our minorities upset and stirred," Fire Captain Beatty explains to underling Montag. "Colored people don't like Little Black Sambo. Burn it. White people don't feel good about Uncle Tom's Cabin. Burn it. Someone's written a book on tobacco and cancer of the lungs? The cigarette people are weeping? Burn the book. Serenity, Montag. Peace, Montag."[53] Book burning, then, is not an exercise in nihilism. It has a social function: harmony, civility, unity.

The stunted humans produced by such a society are displayed in a vapid conversation about a perfunctory election just past. "I think he's one of the nicest-looking men [who] ever became president," exclaims one woman. "Oh, but the man they ran against him! He wasn't much, was he? Kind of small and homely and he didn't shave too close or comb his hair very well."[54] A superficial society where image trumps substance naturally results from the disappearance of books. Art prefaced life.

Bradbury wrote "The Fireman," the 25,000-word novella that morphed into the larger *Fahrenheit 451*, in the basement of UCLA's library over a nine-day explosion of creativity. "I was driven out of my garage by my loving children, who insisted on coming around to the rear window and singing and tapping on the panes," explained Bradbury on the genesis of his visits to UCLA. "Father had to choose between finishing a story or playing with the girls. I chose to play, of course, which endangered the family income. An office had to be found. We couldn't afford one." As he had done in lieu of going to college, Bradbury, in lieu of going to his nonexistent office, went to the library. Paying a dime for every half hour to use the library's coin-operated typewriters, he ultimately spent $9.80 to complete "The Fireman."[55]

Like so many of Bradbury's stories, *Fahrenheit 451* had many incarnations. "The Fireman" story first appeared in *Galaxy* magazine in 1951. Its elongated version was serialized in *Playboy*, starting with Hugh Hefner's second issue. Then came a small run of hardbacks, followed by millions of mass-market paperbacks. It made its way onto the big screen in the 1960s. The cinematic treatment, watchable but generally underwhelming, improved on the original text in one key area. Clarisse, the vivacious teenaged neighbor who catalyzes Montag's reassessment of his book-burning profession, reappears in the land of the living books as a sort of familiar guide for its newest inhabitant. In the book, she disappears with hardly an explanation—perhaps a common enough occurrence in a totalitarian society, but in a novel an unsquared circle that reads more like a draft than a finished product.

More ironic revisions occurred when the publisher Ballantine, in an effort to market the book for high-school classrooms, deleted expletives, references to mature themes, and controversial words and phrases. The nonauthoritative emendations to a book ostensibly about censorship proved too much for the author. In 1979, Ballantine, after printing the bowdlerized version for more than a decade, reset *Fahrenheit 451* to its original type.[56]

There are more than five million copies of *Fahr-*

enheit 451 in circulation. The book has never been out of print because it has always felt relevant. Indifference to books, minority pressures to limit speech, escapism through drugs and suicide, and state intrusiveness have grown since Bradbury's book about such concerns was published in 1953. More than a half century after its first printing, this story about an alternative future uncannily still reads of the here and now.

By the Book

Ray Bradbury didn't study creative writing or literature at a top university. He was unable to afford college. He went to the library instead for three days a week—later proudly claiming the Los Angeles Public Library as his alma mater.[57] The wannabe author read and wrote, and wrote, and wrote. Immersing himself in books made him an intellectual; doing so at the public library made him a blue-collar intellectual.

Privation, not a trust fund, propelled his writing. Between 1943 and 1962, he published 239 stories.[58] Bradbury's midcentury creative explosion coincided with a new wife, the addition of four daughters, and a lateral move into writing from the equally esteemed occupation of street-corner newspaper barker. But according to the prolific author, he wrote to write rather than to eat. "With me, poverty had nothing to do with writing so many stories. I've always had a lust for life, for art, for the written word and I simply *had* to write each and every day, whether stories sold or not."[59]

He wrote to write. He also wrote to be read. This meant writing for a mass audience increasingly more interested in watching than reading. The man who exiled television from his home feverishly peddled his stories for broadcast, recognizing that the remainder of the population didn't enthusiastically share his literary pastimes. Good literature was too important to be left atop the shelf. In fact, given that pulp and slick magazines, rather than books, generally gave birth to the tales, their lives outside the book is consistent with their origins.

Take "The Black Ferris." It began life in pulp fiction in a 1948 number of *Weird Tales*. Several comic books adapted the story. NBC used it in 1956 as the pilot for its ill-fated *Sneak Preview* series, and *The Ray Bradbury Theater* resurrected it in 1990. In the meantime, the short story morphed into a novel, 1962's *Something Wicked This Way Comes*, which itself became the basis of Touchstone's third film in 1983.[60] This is in no way a complete history of its many incarnations but paints enough of a picture to convey that Bradbury's stories were not bound by their book covers. If you didn't look for a Ray Bradbury story, a Ray Bradbury story looked for you.

The medium varied. One message remained consistent: reading is good for your mind. The life of the mind and the literary culture are one and the same. Television? "That insidious beast, that Medusa, which freezes a billion people to stone every night."[61] Surfing the net? "We have too many cellphones. We've got too many Internets. We have got to get rid of those machines."[62] Video games? "That's male ego crap."[63] Books? They raised a poor midwestern geek from obscurity to print immortality. Bradbury could use extratextual media to convey his stories; he couldn't have become a talented writer by relying solely on those media. Only by first reading could he become a writer and provide so much multimedia entertainment.

Bradbury's books glorified books. In *Fahrenheit 451*, outcasts find redemption by becoming great books. In "Long Division," a divorcing couple fights over custody—not of the children but of the family library.[64] "The Exiles" are Earth's last remaining copies of *Dracula*, *An Occurrence at Owl Creek Bridge*, *The Willows*, *A Christmas Carol*, and other tales of the supernatural rocketed to Mars for incineration.[65] Bradbury's oeuvre is a massive, shameless advertisement for further reading. Reading Ray Bradbury is its own encouragement for further reading. Alas, those needing that message most are not generally Ray Bradbury readers.

Horatio Alger stories have diverse beginnings. Intellectual Horatio Alger stories all begin with books.

Notes

Introduction

1. Stephanie Hardiman, "Library's Game to Attract Teen Patrons," *Portland Press Herald*, August 12, 2010, http://www.pressherald.com/news/librarys-game-to-attract-teen-patrons_2010_08_12.html, accessed August 31, 2010.

2. Steven Johnson, *Everything Bad Is Good for You: How Today's Popular Culture Is Actually Making Us Smarter* (New York: Riverhead Books, 2005), 99.

3. Larissa MacFarquhar, "Who Cares If Johnny Can't Read," *Slate*, April 17, 1997, http://www.slate.com/id/3128/, accessed September 21, 2010.

4. Danah Boyd, "Why Youth (Heart) Social Network Sites: The Role of Networked Publics in Teenage Social Life," *MacArthur Foundation Series on Digital Learning—Youth, Identity, and Digital Media Volume*, ed. David Buckingham (Cambridge, MA: MIT Press, 2007), http://www.danah.org/papers/WhyYouthHeart.pdf, accessed September 8, 2010.

5. Johnson, *Everything Bad Is Good for You*, 129.

6. David Silverman, "In Defense of Multitasking," *Harvard Business Review* blog, June 9, 2010, http://blogs.hbr.org/silverman/2010/06/in-defense-of-multitasking.html, accessed September 9, 2010.

7. Susan Jacoby, *The Age of American Unreason* (New York: Pantheon Books, 2008), 259.

8. "Texting Teen Falls Down Open Manhole on Staten Island," MyFoxNY.com, July 11, 2009, http://www.myfoxny.com/dpp/news/local_news/nyc/090710_Texting_Teen_Falls_Down_Open_Manhole, accessed September 8, 2010; "Teen Texts 300,000 Times in Month," KCRA.com, May 5, 2009, http://www.kcra.com/print/19369840/detail.html, accessed August 31, 2010; Adrian Carrasquilo, "Woman Falls into Fountain While Texting, Sues," *Fox News Latino*, January 21, 2011, http://latino.foxnews.com/latino/news/2011/01/21/woman-falls-fountain-texting/, accessed February 8, 2011.

9. U.S. Bureau of Labor Statistics, "Table 11: Time Spent in Leisure and Sports Activities for the Civilian Population by Selected Characteristics, 2009 Annual Averages," http://data.bls.gov/cgi-bin/print.pl/news.release/atus.t11.htm, accessed August 31, 2010.

10. David Abel, "Welcome to the Library. Say Goodbye to the Books," *Boston Globe*, September 4, 2009, 1.

11. Quoted in Nicholas Carr, *The Shallows: What the Internet Is Doing to Our Brains* (New York: W. W. Norton, 2010), 9.

12. Sara Corbett, "Learning by Playing: Video Games in the Classroom," *New York Times Magazine*, September 15, 2010.

13. "Celebrate National Gaming Day @ Your Library," ILoveLibraries.org, http://www.ilovelibraries.org/gaming, accessed August 31, 2010.

14. Bridget Tharp, "Libraries Use Video Games to Attract Teens," *Toledo Blade*, January 6, 2010, http://www.toledoblade.com/frontpage/2010/01/06/Libraries-use-video-games-to-attract-teens.html, accessed June 1, 2011.

15. Ryan Donovan, e-mail interview with author, November 4–5, 2010.

16. Allen Kesinger, e-mail interview with author, November 7–8, 2010.

17. Johnson, *Everything Bad Is Good for You*, 181.

18. Russell Lynes, "Highbrow, Lowbrow, Middlebrow," *Harper's*, February 1949, 19, 21.

19. Dwight Macdonald, "Masscult and Midcult: II," *Partisan Review*, Fall 1960, 614.

20. Virginia Woolf, "To the Editor of the 'New Statesman,'" October 1932, http://hilobrow.com/2009/03/04/woolf-contra-middlebrow/, accessed April 28, 2010.

21. Paul Fussell, *Class: A Guide Through the American Status System* (New York: Summit Books, 1983), 144.

22. Alan D. Sokal, "A Physicist Experiments with Cultural Studies," *Lingua Franca*, May/June 1996, http://www.physics.nyu.edu/faculty/sokal/lingua_franca_v4/lingua_franca_v4.html, accessed September 21, 2010.

23. Jacoby, *The Age of American Unreason*, 107.

24. W. A. Pannapacker, "Confessions of a Middlebrow Professor," *Chronicle Review*, October 5, 2009, http://chronicle.com/article/Confessions-of-a-Middlebrow/48644/, accessed April 26, 2010.

Chapter 1
The Apostate Historians

1. *The Age of Napoleon* entered the *New York Times* best-seller list on December 14, 1975, and remained through January 25, 1976.

2. Quoted in Raymond A. Schroth, S.J., "Will Durant's Religion: Seminary, Exile, 'Return,'" *New Jersey History* (Spring/Summer 1993): 45–64.

3. Paul Avrich, *The Modern School: Anarchism and Education in the United States* (Princeton, NJ: Princeton University Press, 1980), 81–99; Will Durant, *Transition: A Sentimental Story of One Mind and One Era* (New York: Simon and Schuster, 1927), 197–99.

4. Will and Ariel Durant, *A Dual Autobiography* (New York: Simon and Schuster, 1977), 51–52.

5. Will and Ariel Durant, *A Dual Autobiography*, 46; Avrich, *The Modern School*, 99–106.

6. Herbert Mitgang, "Ariel Durant, Historian, Is Dead: Wrote 'The Story of Civilization,'" *New York Times*, October 28, 1981, B4; "Historian Will Durant Dies: Author of 'Civilization' Series," *New York Times*, November 9, 1981, 1, B14; Avrich, *The Modern School*, 99–102.

7. Will Durant, *Transition*, 240.

8. Avrich, *The Modern School*, 196–208.

9. Will Durant, *Transition*, 211–12; Will and Ariel Durant, *A Dual Autobiography*, 57; "History as a River," *Time*, September 28, 1953, 88–90.

10. "Tragedy," *Woman Rebel*, July 1914, 33; Robert A. Thorpe, "A Defense of Assassination," *Woman Rebel*, July 1914, 33. For a description of Sanger's flight from prosecution, see Ellen Chesler, *Woman of Valor and the Birth Control Movement in America* (New York: Simon and Schuster, 1992), 102–40.

11. Irwin Granich, "The Three Whose Hatred Killed Them," *The Masses*, August 1914, 11. After illegally avoiding the draft for the First World War, Granich changed his name to Mike Gold.

12. Avrich, *The Modern School*, 195–206.

13. Will Durant, *Transition*, 213.

14. Ibid., 238.

15. Joan Shelley Rubin, *The Making of Middlebrow Culture* (Chapel Hill, NC: University of North Carolina Press, 1992), 222; Will and Ariel Durant, *A Dual Autobiography*, 37–40, 42–43, 54, 86–87, 117–18.

16. Will and Ariel Durant, *A Dual Autobiography*, 68–69; Will Durant, *Transition*, 263–66, 316–20.

17. Will and Ariel Durant, *A Dual Autobiography*, 59.

18. "Church Services Tomorrow," *New York Times*, February 8, 1919, 19; "Church Services Tomorrow," *New York Times*,

May 31, 1919, 13; "Church Services Tomorrow," *New York Times*, June 14, 1919, 22; "Church Services Tomorrow," *New York Times*, September 20, 1919, 23.

19. "In the Current Week," *New York Times*, December 10, 1922, 34; "In the Current Week," *New York Times*, September 28, 1924, E6; "In the Current Week," *New York Times*, October 23, 1921, 30; "In the Current Week," *New York Times*, April 13, 1924, E3; "In the Current Week," *New York Times*, May 8, 1921, 37.

20. Will and Ariel Durant, *A Dual Autobiography*, 95–96; Robert W. Merry, "The Age of the Durants," WillDurant.com, http://www.willdurant.com/observer.htm, accessed April 22, 2009; Elliot Shore, *Talkin' Socialism: J. A. Wayland and the Radical Press* (Lawrence, KS: University of Kansas Press, 1988), 219–26.

21. Robert Van Gelder, "A Publisher Talks about His Enthusiasms," *New York Times*, November 10, 1940, 102.

22. Rubin, *The Making of Middlebrow Culture*, 247.

23. Ibid., 246, 249.

24. Simon and Schuster, "The Story of Philosophy—*First!*," advertisement in the *New York Times*, November 21, 1926, BR19.

25. Simon and Schuster, "A Tribute to the Intellectual Curiosity of the American Public!," advertisement in the *New York Times*, January 23, 1927, BR15.

26. Michael Korda, *Making the List: A Cultural History of the American Bestseller, 1900–1999* (New York: Barnes and Noble, 2001), 50–53, 64. For 1926–27 and 1930, *The Story of Philosophy* made the annual top ten. Durant's *Mansions of Philosophy* landed at number ten for 1929. According to a study printed in *Publishers Weekly*, *The Story of Philosophy* was the third best-selling nonfiction book in the years between 1920 and 1932 ("Book on Diet Led Non-Fiction Sales," *New York Times*, February 6, 1933, 6.).

27. Rubin, *The Making of Middlebrow Culture*, 244.

28. Will and Ariel Durant, *A Dual Autobiography*, 103.

29. Ibid.

30. Will Durant, *The Story of Philosophy: The Lives and Opinions of the Great Philosophers of the Western World* (New York: Simon and Schuster, 1926, 1961), v–vi.

31. Conrad Wesselhoeft, "St. Peter's Fills Will and Ariel Durant Chair in Humanities," *New York Times*, December 8, 1985, NJ22; Will and Ariel Durant, *A Dual Autobiography*, 47–48.

32. Will and Ariel Durant, *A Dual Autobiography*, 105–9.

33. "Will Durant Begins Tour," *New York Times*, January 12, 1930, 31; Will and Ariel Durant, *A Dual Autobiography*, 140–52.

34. Will and Ariel Durant, *A Dual Autobiography*, 179.

35. "Bestsellers Here and Elsewhere," *New York Times*, August 5, 1935, 13; "Bestsellers Here and Elsewhere," *New York Times*, August 12, 1935, 13; "Bestsellers of the Week, Here and Elsewhere," *New York Times*, August 26, 1935, 13; "Bestsellers of the Week, Here and Elsewhere," *New York Times*, September 2, 1935, 15; "Bestsellers of the Week, Here and Elsewhere," *New York Times*, September 9, 1935, 17; "Bestsellers of the Week, Here and Elsewhere," *New York Times*, September 30, 1935, 15; "Bestsellers of the Week, Here and Elsewhere," *New York Times*, October 21, 1935, 17; "Bestsellers of the Week, Here and Elsewhere," *New York Times*, November 11, 1935, 21; "Bestsellers of the Week, Here and Elsewhere," *New York Times*, November 18, 1935, 21; "Bestsellers of the Week, Here and Elsewhere," *New York Times*, December 2, 1935, 21.

36. Will Durant, "Dictatorship over the Proletariat," *Saturday Evening Post*, February 18, 1933, 56–57.

37. Will and Ariel Durant, *A Dual Autobiography*, 176.

38. Steven K. Gragert and Jane Johansson, eds., *The Papers of Will Rogers: The Final Years, August 1928–August 1935* (Norman, OK: University of Oklahoma Press, 2006), 393n.

39. John Reed, *Ten Days That Shook the World* (1919; repr., New York: Bantam Books, 1988), 188 ("On earth they were

building a kingdom more bright than any heaven had to offer, and for which it was a glory to die"); Christian, "The Rumor in Russia," *The Nation*, December 21, 1918, 766 ("The revolution in Russia is to establish the Kingdom of Heaven here on earth, now; in order that Christ may come soon, and, coming, reign forever")—"Christian" served as a nom de plume for Lincoln Steffens on this occasion; W. E. B. Du Bois, "Russia, 1926," in *W. E. B. Du Bois: A Reader*, ed. David Levering Lewis (New York: Henry Holt, 1995), 582 ("I stand in astonishment and wonder at the revelation of Russia that has come to me").

40. Will Durant, "Dictatorship Over the Proletariat," 56.

41. Will and Ariel Durant, *A Dual Autobiography*, 176.

42. Ibid., 77, 177.

43. Will Durant, *The Life of Greece* (New York: Simon and Schuster, 1939), 56.

44. Will Durant, *Caesar and Christ* (New York: Simon and Schuster, 1944), 665.

45. Will and Ariel Durant, *The Age of Reason Begins* (New York: Simon and Schuster, 1961), 267.

46. Will Durant, *The Renaissance* (New York: Simon and Schuster, 1953), 624.

47. Will and Ariel Durant, *The Age of Reason Begins*, 612.

48. Will Durant, *The Reformation* (New York: Simon and Schuster, 1957), 229.

49. Will Durant, *Caesar and Christ*, 36n.

50. Will Durant, *The Age of Faith*, 1085.

51. Will Durant, *Our Oriental Heritage* (New York: Simon and Schuster, 1935), 558.

52. Will Durant, *The Life of Greece*, 335n.

53. Will and Ariel Durant, *The Age of Reason Begins*, 549.

54. Will Durant, *Our Oriental Heritage*, 131.

55. Ibid., 842–43; Will Durant, *The Reformation*, 694.

56. Will and Ariel Durant, *A Dual Autobiography*, 346–47.

57. Ibid., 153–54, 197–98, 298–99, 394–96.

58. Ibid., 68–71, 206, 212, 219, 373.

59. Ibid., 214, 219.

60. Ibid., 33n, 130–31, 189, 208–9, 234.

61. "Camp Utopia," advertisement in the *New York Times*, June 22, 1924, X13.

62. Will and Ariel Durant, *A Dual Autobiography*, 366.

63. "Historian Will Durant Dies: Author of 'Civilization' Series," 1, B14; "Century of Faith and Fire," *Time*, September 8, 1961, 85–86; "The Essence of the Centuries," *Time*, August 13, 1965, 48–49; Merry, "The Age of the Durants"; Will and Ariel Durant, *A Dual Autobiography*, 182–84, 192, 248.

64. Quoted in Merry, "The Age of the Durants."

65. Simon and Schuster, "A New Masterwork in Will and Ariel Durant's Great 'Story of Civilization,'" advertisement in the *New York Times Book Review*, 14–15.

66. J. H. Plumb, "Some Personalities on the Paths of History," *New York Times Book Review*, September 15, 1963, 3, 44.

67. Henry James Forman, "Will Durant Takes All Civilization as His Province," *New York Times*, August 4, 1935, BR3.

68. John Day, "History—and Dr. Durant—March On," *New York Times*, December 10, 1944, BR4; "Old Rome and the U.S.A.," *Time*, November 27, 1944, 99–100.

69. Orville Prescott, "Books of the Times," *New York Times*, October 23, 1950, 21.

70. "Century of Faith and Fire," 85–86.

71. "A Great March," *Time*, October 6, 1967, 118.

72. "Ariel Durant, Teamed with Husband to Write 'Story of Civilization,'" *Washington Post*, October 27, 1981, B6.

73. Quoted in "Historian Remembered at Quiet Service," Associated Press, November 13, 1981.

Chapter 2
The People's Professor

1. Mortimer J. Adler, *Philosopher at Large: An Intellectual Biography* (New York: Macmillan, 1977), 89. Adler's con-

tempt for *The Story of Philosophy* helped set the tone for his stormy tenure at the University of Chicago, where, upon his hiring, Adler refused to teach an introductory philosophy course because it used Will Durant's biography-driven bestseller as a text. William H. McNeill, *Hutchins' University: A Memoir of the University of Chicago, 1929–1950* (Chicago: University of Chicago Press, 1991), 36.

2. Mortimer J. Adler, "Sleight of Hand," *The Nation*, September 29, 1926, 298–99.

3. "The Idea of Freedom," *Time*, September 22, 1958, 56; Nelson Algren quoted in William Grimes, "Mortimer Adler, 98, Dies; Helped Create Study of Classics," *New York Times*, June 29, 2001, 8.

4. Adler, *Philosopher at Large*, 107.

5. Michael Korda, *Making the List: A Cultural History of the American Bestseller, 1900–1999* (New York: Barnes and Noble, 2001), 88.

6. Ralph McInerny, "Adler on Freedom," in Mortimer J. Adler, *A Second Look in the Rearview Mirror: Further Autobiographical Reflections of a Philosopher at Large* (New York: Macmillan, 1992), 259.

7. Adler, *Philosopher at Large*, 28–29.

8. Ibid., 127–49; McNeill, *Hutchins' University*, 34–38; Amy Apfel Kass, "Radical Conservatives for Liberal Education" (dissertation, Johns Hopkins University, 1973), 118; Tim Lacy, "Making a Democratic Culture" (dissertation, Loyola University Chicago, 2006), 124–34.

9. Adler, *Philosopher at Large*, 139–40. A slightly different account of Stein's verbal barrage is found in "Fusilier," *Time*, March 17, 1952, 82.

10. William Benton, letter to Maurice B. Mitchell, March 22, 1965 (Mortimer Adler Papers, University of Chicago Special Collections [hereafter UCSC], Box 2).

11. Mortimer Adler, letter to Henry Simon, August 27, 1964 (Syracuse University Special Collections, Mortimer Adler Papers, Box 1).

12. Mortimer J. Adler, "Why I Went to College," unpublished manuscript, July 1942, 4 (Mortimer Adler Papers, UCSC, Box 23); Letter: Jasper Spock to Mortimer J. Adler, March, 1, 1943 (Mortimer Adler Papers, UCSC, Box 23). Spock, of George T. Bye and Company, explains of "Why I Went to College": "This has been to Reader's Digest, Saturday Evening Post, American, Good Housekeeping, Atlantic Monthly, This Week, Liberty, Harper's Magazine, Woman's Home Companion, and American Mercury." Alas, all passed.

13. Samuel Eliot Morison, *Three Centuries of Harvard: 1636–1936* (Cambridge, MA: Belknap Press of Harvard University Press, 1936, 1963), 389–90.

14. Lacy, "The Making of a Democratic Culture," 48.

15. Adler, *Philosopher at Large*, 21.

16. "Fusilier," 78–81; Adler, *Philosopher at Large*, 124; Adler, *A Second Look in the Rearview Mirror*, 13.

17. John Erskine, *The Memory of Certain Persons* (Philadelphia: J. B. Lippincott, 1947), 311–37, 342–43; Lacy, "The Making of a Democratic Culture," 71–75.

18. John Erskine, *The Delight of Great Books* (Indianapolis: Bobbs-Merrill, 1928), 11.

19. Kass, "Radical Conservatives for Liberal Education," 6.

20. For a detailed description of the efforts of the world's wealthiest man to establish a great university in Chicago, see, Ron Chernow, *Titan: The Life of John D. Rockefeller Sr.* (New York: Random House, 1998), 299–329.

21. Harry S. Ashmore, *Unseasonable Truths: The Life of Robert Maynard Hutchins* (Boston: Little, Brown, 1989), 27; Alex Beam, *A Great Idea at the Time: The Rise, Fall, and Curious Afterlife of the Great Books* (New York: PublicAffairs, 2008), 29.

22. "Mortimer Adler's Remarks at New Orleans Session, Educational Sales," 1949, 25 (Mortimer Adler Papers, UCSC, Box 4).

23. Robert Hutchins, *The Higher Learning in America* (New Brunswick, NJ: Transaction, 1936, 1995), 110–12, 33–58, 59–87, 31–32, 36.

24. Sydney Hyman, *The Lives of William Benton* (Chicago: University of Chicago, 1969), 286.

25. Lacy, "The Making of a Democratic Culture," 165, 165n. Who broached the idea of an index is disputed. Adler writes of "my suggestion of an idea index," in Adler, *Philosopher at Large*, 239. Benton's biographer credits his subject in Hyman, *The Lives of William Benton*, 287.

26. "The Most Beautiful and Most Useful Home Library Ever Assembled," Great Books of the Western World, Chicago, IL, undated flyer (Mortimer Adler Papers, UCSC, Box 4).

27. Lacy, "The Making of a Democratic Culture," 188n.

28. Erskine, *The Memory of Certain Persons*, 343; Lacy, "The Making of a Democratic Culture," 181–82, 182n.

29. Clifton Fadiman, memo to Mortimer J. Adler, "GBWW, New Edition, Memo #1: Eliminations and Editions," January 4, 1988 (Mortimer Adler Papers, UCSC, Box 123).

30. Robert Hutchins, Preface, *Great Books of the Western World, Volume 1: The Great Conversation*, ed. Robert Maynard Hutchins (New York: Encyclopedia Britannica, 1952), xviii; Adler, *Philosopher at Large*, 240.

31. Quoted in Lacy, "The Making of a Democratic Culture," 197.

32. Dwight Macdonald, "The Book-of-the-Millennium Club," *The New Yorker*, November 29, 1952, 177–78.

33. "The Great Ideas," *Time*, April 24, 1950, 88.

34. Adler, *Philosopher at Large*, 239.

35. Hyman, *The Lives of William Benton*, 393–94.

36. "Production Schedules on Great Books," December 20, 1947 (Mortimer Adler Papers, UCSC, Box 43).

37. William Benton, memo to Mortimer Adler, July 15, 1949 (Mortimer Adler Papers, UCSC, Box 44).

38. Adler, *Philosopher at Large*, 255.

39. Mortimer Adler, letter to Bert, July 31, 1949 (Mortimer Adler Papers, UCSC, Box 44).

40. George Bryson, letter to (blank), September 8, 1950 (Mortimer Adler Papers, UCSC, Box 44); Adler, *Philosopher at Large*, 255–56.

41. R. C. Preble, letter to Mortimer Adler, May 7, 1951 (Mortimer Adler Papers, UCSC, Box 43); George W. Bryson, "Progress Report on 'Great Books' as of October 8, 1951" (Mortimer Adler Papers, UCSC, Box 44).

42. M. J. Adler, letter to James Colvin, November 1, 1951 (Mortimer Adler Papers, UCSC, Box 45); "The Great Ideas: An NBC Radio Discussion by Clare Boothe Luce and Mortimer J. Adler," *The University of Chicago Round Table*, Number 637, June 11, 1950, 1–12 (Mortimer Adler Papers, UCSC, Box 4); "Summary of Meeting on Publicizing the Great Books, June 11, 1947" (Mortimer Adler Papers, UCSC, Box 45).

43. "The Great Ideas," *The University of Chicago Round Table*, 11.

44. James Colvin, Encyclopedia Britannica Inter Office Correspondence to R. C. Preble, November 2, 1951 (Mortimer Adler Papers, UCSC, Box 45).

45. "Fusilier," 76–84.

46. For an example of the numbers fetish of the postwar years, see Mortimer Adler, memo to William Benton, April 1, 1950 (Mortimer Adler Papers, UCSC, Box 4).

47. "An Imaginative Literary Venture into the Sphere of Human Ideas," brochure, *Great Books of the Western World*, Chicago, IL (Mortimer Adler Papers, UCSC, Box 4).

48. Mortimer Adler, memo to William Benton, "In re: Comparison of Harvard Classics and Great Books of the Western World," April 1, 1950 (Mortimer Adler Papers, UCSC, Box 4).

49. "Do the Harvard Classics Meet Today's Demand for Great Books?" poster (Mortimer Adler Papers, UCSC, Box 4).

50. "The Harvard Classics and the Idexicon," advertisement (Mortimer Adler Papers, UCSC, Box 4).

51. Mortimer Adler, "Talk to Sales Promotion Staff, July 1959" (Mortimer Adler Papers, UCSC, Box 4). See also "Mortimer Adler's Remarks at New Orleans Session, Educational Sales," 27. Therein, Adler professes: "By the way, it's very important to notice, the phrase 'classics' has all but

dropped out; even Mr. Black of the Classics Club now uses the phrase 'Great Books.' 'Classics' should drop out because it has the wrong connotation; it means 'antiquity,' you see.'"

52. "Mortimer Adler's Remarks at New Orleans Session, Educational Sales"; Mortimer Adler, "Talk to Sales Promotion Staff, July 1959"; M. J. Adler, letter to James Colvin, November, 1, 1951 (Mortimer Adler Papers, UCSC, Box 4); K. M. Harden, letter to "All Great Books Division Managers," "Division Managers Conference October 15, 16, and 17, 1962," September 17, 1962 (Mortimer Adler Papers, UCSC, Box 4); Mortimer J. Adler, letter to Roger Graver, September 1, 1959 (Mortimer Adler Papers, UCSC, Box 4); "Great Books Meeting," January 13, 1961 (Mortimer Adler Papers, UCSC, Box 4); "Great Books Meeting," February 10, 1961 (Mortimer Adler Papers, UCSC, Box 4).

53. Lacy, "The Making of a Democratic Culture," 180.

54. Mortimer J. Adler, letter to unaddressed, undated (Mortimer Adler Papers, UCSC, Box 44); R. C. Preble, letter to William Benton, May 7, 1951 (Mortimer Adler Papers, UCSC, Box 44). Preble's letter addresses paper shortages, among other matters, and contains a handwritten (presumably from Benton) directive to pass along the missive to "MJA." Adler was also cc'd here.

55. Institute for Philosophical Research, press release, June 12, 1952 (Mortimer Adler Papers, UCSC, Box 11). For an idea of Adler's honoraria and the accompanying speeches, see the folder entitled "Lecture Contracts and Receipts—1951–1952" (Mortimer Adler Papers, UCSC, Box 10). Adler, *Philosopher at Large*, 192–94.

56. Harvey Flaumenhaft, phone interview with author, February 23, 2011. Adler relays that after a respite from speaking at St. John's in the early 1940s, "I have managed to visit the college at least once a year since then." He describes his adventures in lecture halls at St. John's in Adler, *Philosopher at Large*, 212–13.

57. Adler, *Philosopher at Large*, 231–32.

58. Otto A. Bird, Sue Montgomery, and Marlys G. Allen, eds., "Bibliography of Mortimer J. Adler," in Adler, *A Second Look in the Rearview Mirror*, 303–6.

59. "Cashing in on Culture," *Time*, April 20, 1962, 94; "Fusilier," 84.

60. Mortimer Adler, letter to Arthur, November 30, (year undated) (Mortimer Adler Papers, UCSC, Box 53). Therein, Adler discusses his desire to obtain a divorce without divulging his affair. Mortimer Adler, letter to "My beloved" (Sue), November 2–3, (year undated) (Mortimer Adler Papers, UCSC, Box 53). Mortimer Adler to Frank, June 20, 1959, Box 59 (Mortimer Adler Papers, UCSC, Box 59). "Sue and I are very much in love, and have been for some time, but we are *not* married," Adler writes. "I regret very much the imposture we practiced, and I hope that Marian and you will find yourselves able to forgive us for it. . . . There are, extenuating circumstances; and we are both hoping that our situation may be rectified. Sue is not married, and I am." Helen Adler, letter to Mortimer J. Adler, October 17, (year undated) (Mortimer Adler Papers, UCSC, Box 53). See also Adler, *Philosopher at Large*, 236, 282.

61. "Cashing in on Culture," 94.

62. Preble, letter to Adler, May 7, 1951.

63. Adler, *Philosopher at Large*, 237.

64. "An Awareness and Motivation Study of Owners and Prospects for Great Books" (Chicago: Marplan, 1962), 16–17, 19 (Mortimer Adler Papers, UCSC, Box 4).

65. Ibid., 20–21.

66. Ibid., 22–23.

67. Ibid., 76–77.

68. Ibid., 93.

69. Ibid., 92.

70. Ibid., 48–49.

71. Ibid., 70.

72. Ibid., 84–85.

73. "Cashing in on Culture," 94.

74. Adler, letter to Graver, September 1, 1959.

75. Beam, *A Great Idea at the Time*, 107–10.

76. Hyman, *The Lives of William Benton*, 249–62; Beam, *A Great Idea at the Time*, 114–15.

77. Adler, *Philosopher at Large*, 259.

78. Hutchins, ed., *The Great Books of the Western World: Volume 1*, xi.

79. Ibid., 18.

80. Ernest La France, "Winchester and the Great Books," *Parade*, August 1, 1948, 5–7; Ashmore, *Unseasonable Truths*, 273–74.

81. Marlys G. Allen, memo to Members of the Great Books Class, "Re: Great Books Class, May 25, 1988," May 20, 1988 (Mortimer Adler Papers, UCSC, Box 9); Orly Telisman, e-mail correspondence with the author, June 24, 2011. Quoted in Beam, *A Great Idea at the Time*, 142–46.

83. Adler, *A Second Look in the Rearview Mirror*, 215–19.

84. The Ultimate Warrior, phone interview with author, April 14, 2010.

85. Adler, *A Second Look in the Rearview Mirror*, 261; Adler, *Philosopher at Large*, 221–28; Lacy, "The Making of a Democratic Culture," 316n.

86. *Time*, March 17, 1952.

87. Mortimer J. Adler, "What Every Schoolboy Doesn't Know," *Coronet*, January 1944, 88 (Mortimer Adler Papers, UCSC, Box 26).

88. Dwight Macdonald, "Appendix: The Hard Sell," *The Literature & Culture of the American 1950s*, undated, http://www.writing.upenn.edu/~afilreis/50s/macdonald-great-books.html, accessed June 23, 2011.

89. Beam, *A Great Idea at the Time*, 3.

90. Emily Eakin, "More Ado (Yawn) about Great Books," *New York Times* (Education Life Supplement), April 8, 2001, 24.

91. "Mortimer Adler's Remarks at New Orleans Session, Educational Sales."

92. Matthew Arnold, *Culture and Anarchy* (New York: Mac-Millan, 1869, 1892), xi.

Chapter 3
Free-Market Evangelist

1. Milton Friedman and Rose D. Friedman, *Two Lucky People* (Chicago: University of Chicago Press, 1998), 184.
2. Ibid., xii.
3. Ibid., 19–28.
4. Milton Friedman, "The Methodology of Positive Economics," in *Essays in Positive Economics* (Chicago: University of Chicago Press, 1966), 8.
5. Milton Friedman and George J. Stigler, *Roofs or Ceilings? The Current Housing Problem*, September 1946, http://fee.org/library/books/roofs-or-ceilings-the-current-housing-problem/print, accessed July 30, 2010.
6. "Editor's Note," in ibid.
7. Friedman and Friedman, *Two Lucky People*, 151.
8. Quoted in Jennifer Burns, *Goddess of the Market: Ayn Rand and the American Right* (New York: Oxford University Press, 2009), 116–19.
9. Friedman and Friedman, *Two Lucky People*, 150.
10. Ibid., xii.
11. Barry Goldwater, letter to Milton Friedman, July 13, 1962 (Milton Friedman Papers, Hoover Archives, Box 21).
12. Milton Friedman, *Capitalism and Freedom* (Chicago: University of Chicago, 1962, 1982), vi.
13. Roger W. Shugg, letter to Milton Friedman, July 30, 1962 (Milton Friedman Papers, Hoover Archives, Box 232).
14. George H. Nash, *The Conservative Intellectual Movement in America Since 1945* (Wilmington, DE: ISI Books, 1996), 268, 270.
15. Friedman, *Capitalism and Freedom*, 182–89, 35–36, 1–2, 108–18.

16. Ibid., 12.

17. Ibid., 188.

18. Barry Goldwater, *The Conscience of a Conservative* (Washington, DC: Regnery Gateway, 1960, 1990), 17.

19. Friedman and Friedman, *Two Lucky People*, 119–24; Lanny Ebenstein, *Milton Friedman: A Biography* (New York: Palgrave Macmillan, 2007), 43–44.

20. David Friedman, phone interview with author, May 5, 2010.

21. Friedman, *Capitalism and Freedom*, 89.

22. For a primer on school choice, albeit from an interested party, see Clint Bolick, *Voucher Wars: Waging the Legal Battle over School Choice* (Washington, DC: Cato Institute, 2003). See also Milton Friedman, "Free to Choose," *Wall Street Journal*, June 9, 2005, http://online.wsj.com/article/SB111827769927654908.html?mod=2–1239–1, accessed March 12, 2010.

23. Friedman, *Capitalism and Freedom*, 8.

24. Ibid., 7–21, 2–3.

25. Ibid., 197–98.

26. Milton Friedman, letter to Roger Shugg, March 12, 1964 (Milton Friedman Papers, Hoover Archives, Box 232). A week after Friedman's missive, an offended sales manager from the University of Chicago Press wrote Friedman that "your letter is unfair to us" and "your letter is upsetting." William A. Wood, letter to Milton Friedman, March 19, 1964 (Milton Friedman Papers, Hoover Archives, Box 232).

27. "A Tract for the Times," *The Economist*, February 16, 1963, 611.

28. Roger Shugg, letter to Milton Friedman, July 24, 1962; Roger Shugg, letter to Milton Friedman, July 30, 1962 (Milton Friedman Papers, Hoover Archives, Box 232).

29. "Theorizing for Goldwater?" *Business Week*, November 23, 1963, 106; "Right Face," *Newsweek*, January 13, 1964, 73.

30. Jacob J. Kaufman, letter to Phoenix Books, June 15, 1964 (Milton Friedman Papers, Hoover Archives, Box 220).

31. Henry Hazlitt, letter to Milton Friedman, March 16, 1984 (Milton Friedman Papers, Hoover Archives, Box 228).

32. Osborn Elliott, letter to Milton Friedman, July 14, 1966; Milton Friedman, letter to Osborn Elliott, July 26, 1966 (Milton Friedman Papers, Hoover Archives, Box 228); Friedman and Friedman, *Two Lucky People*, 357.

33. Milton Friedman, "Minimum-Wage Rates," *Newsweek*, September 26, 1966, 96.

34. Milton Friedman, "Legislating Unemployment," *Newsweek*, July 3, 1972, 66.

35. Friedman's view of vouchers was complex. "'Your World' Interview with Economist Milton Friedman," FoxNews.com, November 16, 1006, http://www.foxnews.com/printer-friendly_story/0,3566,230045,00.html, accessed March 12, 2010. Therein, Friedman opines: "Vouchers are a means, not an end. The end and the objective is to get an effective educational system." Brian Doherty, "Best of Both Worlds," *Reason*, June 1995, http://reason.com/archives/1995/06/01/best-of-both-worlds/print, accessed March 10, 2010.

36. Milton Friedman, "Negative Income Tax-II," *Newsweek*, October 7, 1968, 92. Therein, Friedman states: "I see the voucher as a step in moving away from a government system to a private system."

37. Milton Friedman, "A New Holiday," *Newsweek*, August 5, 1974, 56.

38. Milton Friedman, "Can We Halt Leviathan?" *Newsweek*, November 6, 1972, 98. Rather than deriving straight from Friedman, Ronald Reagan's famous inauguration line had been used by him for years prior to his inauguration. It may be the case that some variation on that theme was conservative boilerplate. See Michael Scherer and Michael Duffy, "The Role Model: What Obama Sees in Reagan," *Time*, January 27, 2011, http://www.time.com/time/politics/article/0,8599,2044579,00.html, accessed February 9, 2011.

39. "We Are All Keynesians Now," *Time*, December 31, 1965, 65.

40. Milton Friedman, "Fiscal Responsibility," *Newsweek*, August 7, 1967, 68.

41. Friedman's criticism of Arthur Burns's Fed was tenacious. Examples include: Milton Friedman, "Money Explodes," *Newsweek*, May 3, 1971, 81; Milton Friedman, "The Inflationary Fed," *Newsweek*, August 27, 1973, 74; Milton Friedman, "How to Hit the Money Target," *Newsweek*, December 8, 1975, 85; and Milton Friedman, "What Is the Federal Reserve Doing?," *Newsweek*, March 10, 1975, 63. For criticism of Nixon, see Milton Friedman, "What the President Should Have Done," *Newsweek*, July 16, 1973, 72. For columns critical of Reagan, see Milton Friedman, "Protection That Hurts," *Newsweek*, November 15, 1982, 90; and Milton Friedman, "'No' to More Money for the IMF," *Newsweek*, November 14, 1983, 96.

42. Milton Friedman, "The Kemp-Roth Free Lunch," *Newsweek*, August 7, 1978, 59.

43. Milton Friedman, "A Volunteer Army," *Newsweek*, December 19, 1966, 100. For a short history of Friedman's role in ending conscription, see David R. Henderson, "The Role of Economists in Ending the Draft," *Econ Journal Watch*, August 2005, 362–74.

44. Dr. J. E. Schmidt, letter to Milton Friedman, June 15, 1969 (Milton Friedman Papers, Hoover Archives, Box 228).

45. Milton Friedman, "Prohibition and Drugs," *Newsweek*, May 1, 1972, 104.

46. Milton Friedman, "Frustrating Drug Advancement," *Newsweek*, January 8, 1973, 49.

47. Friedman and Friedman, *Two Lucky People*, 363.

48. Ardie Lubin, letter to Milton Friedman, January 3, 1973 (Milton Friedman Papers, Hoover Archives, Box 229).

49. Friedman and Friedman, *Two Lucky People*, 362.

50. Milton Friedman, "Barking Cats," *Newsweek*, February 19, 1973, 70.

51. "The Negro in America: What Must Be Done," *Newsweek*, November 20, 1967, 32–65; Milton Friedman, "The Negro in America," *Newsweek*, December 11, 1967, 89.

52. Osborn Elliott, letter to Milton Friedman, November 30, 1967; Milton Friedman, letter to Osborn Elliott, December 12, 1967 (Milton Friedman Papers, Hoover Archives, Box 228).

53. Milton Friedman, letter to Osborn Elliott, October 23, 1968; Osborn Elliott, letter to Milton Friedman, November 8, 1968; Milton Friedman, letter to Osborn Elliott, December 10, 1968; Osborn Elliott, letter to Milton Friedman, January 7, 1969 (Milton Friedman Papers, Hoover Archives, Box 228).

54. Milton Friedman, letter to Lawrence Martz, May 6, 1968 (Milton Friedman Papers, Hoover Archives, Box 228).

55. Milton Friedman, letter to Lawrence Martz, July 5, 1978 (Milton Friedman Papers, Hoover Archives, Box 228).

56. Brian Domitrovic, *Econoclasts: The Rebels Who Sparked the Supply-Side Revolution and Restored American Prosperity* (Wilmington, DE: ISI Books, 2009), 103.

57. Friedman, "Inflationary Recession," *Newsweek*, October 17, 1967, 92.

58. Milton Friedman, "Marx and Money," *Newsweek*, October 27, 1980, 95; Milton Friedman, "Defining 'Monetarism,'" *Newsweek*, July 12, 1982, 64.

59. Friedman, "Steady as You Go," *Newsweek*, January 10, 1977, 58.

60. Milton Friedman, "Boycotts and Prices," *Newsweek*, November 28, 1966, 92.

61. Milton Friedman, "Inflation and Wages," *Newsweek*, September 28, 1970, 77; Milton Friedman, "Implementing Humphrey-Hawkins," *Newsweek*, March 5, 1979, 87.

62. Milton Friedman, letter to William Broyles Jr., December 22, 1983 (Milton Friedman Papers, Hoover Archives, Box 228).

63. Smith wrote: "My decision to discontinue your and Lester Thurow's columns has probably been the toughest I've made since I took over as editor-in-chief two weeks ago." Richard M. Smith, letter to Milton Friedman, January 18, 1984 (Milton Friedman Papers, Hoover Archives, Box 228).

64. Milton Friedman, "A Recession Warning," *Newsweek*, January 16, 1984, 68.

65. Friedman's name appeared as a contributing editor on the masthead as late as the last issue of June 1984 despite his last column appearing in January. "Newsweek," *Newsweek*, June 25, 1984, 9. Milton Friedman, letter to Rudy Boschwitz, May 19, 1984 (Milton Friedman Papers, Hoover Archives, Box 228).

66. Milton Friedman, letter to Kenneth Auchincloss, January 31, 1986 (Milton Friedman Papers, Hoover Archives, Box 228).

67. Bob Chitester, phone interview with author, March 14, 2010.

68. Milton Friedman, letter to Arnold Moore, October 4, 1977 (Milton Friedman Papers, Hoover Archives, Box 224); Peter W. Bernstein, "The Man Who Brought You Milton Friedman," *Fortune*, February 25, 1980, 109.

69. Bob Chitester, phone interview with author, March 14, 2010.

70. Milton Friedman, letter to Robert Chitester, July 26, 1977 (Milton Friedman Papers, Hoover Archives, Box 61).

71. Michael Latham, memo to Michael Peacock, "MF Series Title," January 25, 1979 (Milton Friedman Papers, Hoover Archives, Box 224); Milton Friedman, letter to Anthony Jay, Robert Reid, Michael Peacock, Michael Latham, February 8, 1978 (Milton Friedman Papers, Hoover Archives, Box 224); Bob Chitester, memo to Milton Friedman, "Optional Addition to Capitalism and Freedom Series," January 26, 1977 (Milton Friedman Papers, Hoover Archives, Box 223); "Free: Free to Choose/Promotion and Publicity Plan," WQLN, Public Communications, Inc., February 1979 (Milton Friedman Papers, Hoover Archives, Box 224); Friedman and Friedman, *Two Lucky People*, 496.

72. Robert Chitester, letter to Milton Friedman, October 17, 1977 (Milton Friedman Papers, Hoover Archives, Box 61).

73. Bob Chitester, phone interview with author, March 14, 2010.

74. Robert Chitester, letter to George Shultz, October 7, 1977 (Milton Friedman Papers, Hoover Archives, Box 61).

75. Tony Jay, memo "The Milton Friedman Series," November 14, 1977 (Milton Friedman Papers, Hoover Archives, Box 224); Milton and Rose D. Friedman, *Two Lucky People*, 478–80.

76. Milton Friedman, letter to Anthony Jay and Michael Peacock, December 18, 1977 (Milton Friedman Papers, Hoover Archives, Box 225).

77. Jay, "The Milton Friedman Series."

78. Friedman, letter to Jay and Peacock.

79. Milton Friedman, letter to Terry D. Hill, February 28, 1992 (Milton Friedman Papers, Hoover Archives, Box 224).

80. Video Arts/WQLN, "Free to Choose: From Cradle to Grave" (prod. Michael Latham, 1980); Video Arts/WQLN, "Free to Choose: How to Stay Free" (prod. Michael Latham, 1980); Video Arts/WQLN, "Free to Choose: Created Equal" (prod. Michael Latham, 1980).

81. Milton Friedman and Rose Friedman, *Free to Choose: A Personal Statement* (New York: Harcourt Brace Jovanovich, 1979, 1980), xi–xii; Friedman and Friedman, *Two Lucky People*, 371, 481.

82. Video Arts/WQLN, "Free to Choose: From Cradle to Grave"; Video Arts/WQLN, "Free to Choose: Who Protects the Consumer?" (prod. Michael Latham, 1980); Video Arts/WQLN, "Free to Choose: How to Cure Inflation" (prod. Michael Latham, 1980).

83. Video Arts/WQLN, "Free to Choose: Created Equal."

84. "Economist Slaps PBS Publicly on Eve of His Series," *Cleveland Plain Dealer*, January 13, 1980 (Milton Friedman Papers, Hoover Archives, Box 223).

85. Friedman and Friedman, *Two Lucky People*, 25, 157; Milton Friedman, letter to Jennifer Roback, June 10, 1981 (Milton Friedman Papers, Hoover Archives, Box 231).

86. Friedman and Friedman, *Two Lucky People*, 58.

87. Friedman, letter to Roback.

88. "Now That You've Seen the TV Show," *Fortune*, February 25, 1980, 110. See also "Uncle Miltie," *Time*, March 10, 1980, 71.

89. Milton Friedman, letter to Michael Peacock, January 17, 1978 (Milton Friedman Papers, Hoover Archives, Box 224).

90. "Now That You've Seen the TV Show," 110.

91. Bob Chitester, phone interview with author, March 14, 2010.

92. Michael Korda, *Making the List: A Cultural History of the American Bestseller, 1900–1999* (New York: Barnes and Noble Books, 2001), 175.

93. Roberta Gluzband, letter to Milton Friedman, February 21, 1980; Michael D. Goff, letter to Milton Friedman, January 25, 1980; Mr. and Mrs. Paul Haskell, letter to Milton Friedman, September 13, 1980 (Milton Friedman Papers, Hoover Archives, Box 224).

94. Pat and Bill Bandle, letter to Milton Friedman, March 8, 1980 (Milton Friedman Papers, Hoover Archives, Box 223).

95. Friedman and Friedman, *Two Lucky People*, 498–501; Bob Chitester, phone interview with author, March 14, 2010.

96. Ralph Harris Jr., letter to Milton Friedman, February 5, 1980 (Milton Friedman Papers, Hoover Archives, Box 224).

97. Lawrence H. Summers, "The Great Liberator," *New York Times*, November 19, 2006.

98. Paul Krugman, "Who Was Milton Friedman?," *New York Review of Books*, February 15, 2007, available at http://www.nybooks.com/articles/19857, accessed March 3, 2010.

99. "The Economics of Emissions Offsets Trading," EnergyStocksBlog.com, August 27, 2008, http://www.energystocksblog.com/2008/08/27/the-economics-of-emissions-offsets-trading/, accessed February 25, 2011; Robert H. Frank, "The Other Milton Friedman: A Conservative with a Social Welfare Program," *New York Times*, November 23, 2007, http://www.nytimes.com/2006/11/23/business/23scene.html?pagewanted=print, accessed February 25, 2011; Andy Beckett, "Ready, Ken?" *Guardian* (UK), February 10, 2003,

http://www.guardian.co.uk/politics/2003/feb/10/london.
congestioncharging/print, accessed February 25, 2011.

100. Katherine Mangu-Ward, "The Milton Friedman Show,"
Reason, June 2007, http://www.reason.com/archives/2007/05/01/
the-milton-friedman-show, accessed February 8, 2011.

Chapter 4
The Longshoreman Philosopher

1. Bob Chitester, phone interview with author, March 14,
2010.

2. Thomas Sowell, "The Legacy of Eric Hoffer," *Capitalism
Magazine*, June 19, 2003, http://www.capitalismmagazine.
com/culture/living/people/2868-the-legacy-of-eric-hoffer.
html, accessed June 20, 2011.

3. "From a Letter from Eric Hoffer, December 24, 1949"
(Eric Hoffer Papers, Hoover Archives, Box 25).

4. Eric Hoffer, *Truth Imagined* (New York: Harper & Row,
1983), 3.

5. Ibid., 23–25.

6. Ibid., 25.

7. For examples of the kind of work Hoffer engaged in during
his years as an itinerant worker, see ibid., 26, 45, 53, 68–70,
72–73. For Hoffer's account of his relationship with Berkeley
graduate student "Helen," see ibid., 58–67.

8. Eric Hoffer, "Autobiographical Writing: 1934–1936," 1–2,
7, 13, 19–24 (Eric Hoffer Papers, Hoover Archives, Box 47).

9. Ibid., 5–6.

10. Ibid., 7–9.

11. Ibid., 15.

12. Tom Bethell, "The Longshoreman Philosopher," *Hoover
Digest*, January 30, 2003, http://www.hoover.org/publications/
hoover-digest/article/7854, accessed March 4, 2010.

13. Lili Osborne, interview with author in San Francisco,
California, January 15, 2010.

14. Ibid.

15. Ibid.

16. "February 24, 1946" (Eric Hoffer Collection, San Francisco Public Library, Box 1, Folder 2).

17. Eric Hoffer, *The True Believer: Thoughts on the Nature of Mass Movements* (New York: Harper Perennial Classics, 1951, 2002), iv.

18. Calvin Tomkins, *Eric Hoffer: An American Odyssey* (New York: E. P. Dutton, 1968), 31.

19. Harvey Klehr and John Earl Haynes, "The Comintern's Open Secrets," *American Spectator*, December 1992, 34–36.

20. Eric Hoffer, *Working and Thinking on the Waterfront* (New York: Harper & Row, 1969), 101, 124, 139.

21. Eric Hoffer, "Notebook," March 1949 (Eric Hoffer Collection, San Francisco Public Library, Box 3, Folder 11).

22. Eric Hoffer, "Hoffer, Eric: Notebook: 1949" (Eric Hoffer Collection, San Francisco Public Library, Box 2, Folder 3).

23. KQED, "Conversations with Eric Hoffer: Part 6," San Francisco, 1963–64 (Eric Hoffer Collection, San Francisco Public Library); KQED, "Conversations with Eric Hoffer: Part 7," San Francisco, 1963–64 (Eric Hoffer Collection, San Francisco Public Library).

24. Floyd L. Nourse, letter to Eric Hoffer, March 6, 1951; Simon Michael Bessie, letter to Eric Hoffer, January 7, 1959 (Eric Hoffer Papers, Hoover Archives, Box 30).

25. Lili Osborne, interview with author.

26. KQED, "Conversations with Eric Hoffer: Part 5," San Francisco, 1963–64 (Eric Hoffer Collection, San Francisco Public Library).

27. Eric Hoffer, "Notebook" (Eric Hoffer Collection, San Francisco Public Library, Box 1, Folder 3); Eric Hoffer, "Notebook" (Eric Hoffer Collection, San Francisco Public Library, Box 2, Folder 1); Eric Hoffer, "Notebook," January 1947 (Eric Hoffer Collection, San Francisco Public Library, Box 2, Folder 2); Eric Hoffer, Notebook IV-11, 57 (Eric Hoffer Papers, Hoover Archives, Box 90).

28. Lili Osborne, interview with author.

29. This Hofferism was repeated in various venues, including, conspicuously, on the back inside dust jacket of Eric Hoffer, *Reflections on the Human Condition* (New York: Harper & Row, 1973).

30. Eric Hoffer, *The Passionate State of Mind* (New York: Harper & Row, 1954, 1955), 69.

31. Eric Hoffer, *The Ordeal of Change* (1963; repr. Cutchogue, NY: Buccaneer Books, 1976), 88.

32. Eric Hoffer, *The Temper of Our Time* (New York: Harper & Row, 1967), xi.

33. Eric Hoffer, *Before the Sabbath* (New York: Harper & Row, 1979), 3.

34. Eric Hoffer, "Rudeness, Weapon of the Fanatic," *Los Angeles Times*, July 27, 1969, E7.

35. Hoffer, *The Temper of Our Time*, 51.

36. Hoffer, *Before the Sabbath*, 109–10.

37. Lili Osborne, interview with author.

38. Eric Hoffer, "Notebook 14" (Eric Hoffer Collection, San Francisco Public Library, Box 3, Folder 13).

39. Tomkins, *Eric Hoffer: An American Odyssey*, 35.

40. "Comment by Evan Thomas," undated; "Comment by John Fischer," undated (Eric Hoffer Papers, Hoover Archives, Box 49).

41. Hoffer, *Truth Imagined*, 94.

42. Hoffer, *The True Believer*, xii.

43. Ibid., xiii.

44. Ibid., 91.

45. Ibid., 82.

46. Ibid., 80.

47. Orville Prescott, "Books of the Times," *New York Times*, March 16, 1951, 29; Orville Prescott, "Books of the Times," *New York Times*, January 1, 1960, 17.

48. Bertrand Russell, "How Fanatics Are Made," *The Observer*, March 23, 1952, 4.

49. Marguerite Higgins, "Eisenhower's Other Side," *This Week*, January 25, 1953, 7.

50. "Ike's Favorite Author," *Look*, June 12, 1956, 40.

51. Anthony Leviero, "President Urging a Book to Friends," *New York Times*, March 19, 1956, 12.

52. "Ike's Favorite Philosopher?," *People Today*, May 16, 1956, 38.

53. Dwight Eisenhower, letter to Robert J. Biggs, February 10, 1959, Presidential Papers of Dwight David Eisenhower, Document #1051, http://www.eisenhowermemorial. org/presidential-papers/second-term/documents/1051.cfm, accessed April 22, 2010.

54. For example, see Richard Hofstadter, *Anti-Intellectualism in American Life* (London: Jonathan Cape, 1962, 1964), 3–5.

55. KQED, "Conversations with Eric Hoffer: Part 2," San Francisco, 1963–64 (Eric Hoffer Collection, San Francisco Public Library).

56. Lili Osborne, interview with author.

57. Hoffer, *Working and Thinking on the Waterfront*, 11, 12, 16, 23, 41, 54, 56–57, 60–61, 67, 78, 81, 89, 92, 96, 106, 112, 115, 125, 132–33, 165, 167.

58. Ibid., 6, 7, 12, 67, 89; Eric Hoffer, letter to Eric Osborne, undated (Eric Hoffer Papers, Hoover Archives, Box 36, Folder 14).

59. Jack Fincher, "San Francisco's Longshoreman Philosopher," *Los Angeles Times*, June 11, 1967, L39–40.

60. Tomkins, *Eric Hoffer: An American Odyssey*, 51, 61.

61. Selden Osborne, letter to Eric Hoffer, undated (Eric Hoffer Papers, Hoover Archives, Box 36). For an example of Selden's affection for Hoffer, see Selden Osborne, letter to Eric Hoffer, January 20, 1964 (Eric Hoffer Papers, Hoover Archives, Box 36).

62. Hoffer, *Working and Thinking on the Waterfront*, 60–61.

63. Eric Osborne, letter to Eric Hoffer, undated (Eric Hoffer Papers, Hoover Archives, Box 36).

64. Melville Maddocks, "California's Guru," *Christian Science Monitor*, January 5, 1967, 7; Edmund Fuller, "The Bookshelf: From the Waterfront," *Wall Street Journal*, March 4, 1969, 20.

65. Lili Osborne, letter to Eric Hoffer, undated (Eric Hoffer Papers, Hoover Archives, Box 36).

66. "CBS Will Repeat Interview with Hoffer Nov. 14," *Los Angeles Times*, October 21, 1967, B3; Aileen MacMinn, "Lucille Ball, Don Adams Capture Emmy Awards," *Los Angeles Times*, May 20, 1968, 3.

67. Al Kuettner, "Eric Hoffer: 'She Told Me I Would Die at 40. . . . Now I Am Like a Tourist on This Earth,'" *Chicago Tribune*, January 28, 1968, J22.

68. Eric Sevareid, "Introduction," in Tomkins, *Eric Hoffer: An American Odyssey*, ix–x.

69. Beatrice Small, letter to Eric Hoffer, February 4, 1969; L. W. Jager, letter to Eric Sevareid, February 6, 1969 (Eric Hoffer Papers, Hoover Archives, Box 65).

70. Indecipherable, letter to Eric Hoffer, January 29, 1969 (Eric Hoffer Papers, Hoover Archives, Box 65).

71. "The President: His Kind of Intellectual," *Newsweek*, October 16, 1967, 26; "The Presidency: Consensus of a Different Kind," *Time*, October 13, 1967, 25–26; CBS News, "Eric Hoffer: The Passionate State of Mind" (Prod., Jack Beck, 1967).

72. Tomkins, *Eric Hoffer: An American Odyssey*, 48.

73. Eric Hoffer, "What I Have Learned—IV: A Strategy for the War with Nature," *Saturday Review*, February 5, 1966, 74.

74. "Hoffer Irked, Walks Out on Violence Hearing," *Los Angeles Times*, October 24, 1968, 4; "Hoffer Explodes at Negro Testifying at Violence Probe," *Hartford Courant*, October 26, 1968, 1; Jean White, "Dissent over Protesters Marks Violence Hearing," *Washington Post*, October 24, 1968, 1.

75. Richard M. Cohen, "Hoffer on Colleges: 'Strong Men Needed,'" *Washington Post*, May 10, 1969, 10.

76. Eric Hoffer, "False Cliches about America," *Los Angeles Times*, December 29, 1968, F9; Eric Hoffer, "Plenty of Presidential Timber," *Los Angeles Times*, April 21, 1968, F7; Eric Hoffer, "The Upsurge of the Intellectual," *Los Angeles Times*, May 12, 1968, L7; Eric Hoffer, "Cold War of the Intellectuals," *Los Angeles Times*, February 4, 1968, K7.

77. Hoffer, "Rudeness, Weapon of the Fanatic."

78. CBS News, "Eric Hoffer: The Passionate State of Mind."

79. Hoffer, *Before the Sabbath*, 12–13; Hoffer, *Working and Thinking on the Waterfront*, 58–59.

80. Eric Hoffer, "Pig Heaven vs. Pig Sty," *Los Angeles Times*, June 16, 1968, L7.

81. CBS News, "The Savage Heart: A Conversation with Eric Hoffer" (Prod., Perry Wolff, 1969).

82. Cass Canfield, letter to Eric Hoffer, July 15, 1968 (Eric Hoffer Papers, Hoover Archives, Box 30). Of *Working and Thinking on the Waterfront*, Canfield writes: "The passages that bother me are a few among quite a number dealing with Negroes. It seems to me that considering the Negro problem at this moment and the divisiveness in this country, three or four of your observations might be toned down or qualified a bit." John MacRae, letter to Eric Hoffer, May 31, 1968 (Eric Hoffer Papers, Hoover Archives, Box 30). Therein, regarding *The Temper of Our Time*, MacRae writes: "My feeling is that you have imposed harsher standards for the Negro than for the white." Hoffer's personal notebooks occasionally yielded even harsher observations than his public declarations. In a 1946 notebook, he wrote that "a great count against the American Negro is the fact that with a vast unknown continent west of the Mississippi there were not enough runaway slaves who sought freedom in the mountains and plains. There should have been at least one free Negro community, a nomadic tribe or an agricultural settlement, somewhere in the wild West. Horses have done that much." Eric Hoffer, "Hoffer, Eric: Notebook, 1946" (Eric Hoffer Collection, San Francisco Public Library, Box 3, Folder 1).

83. CBS News, "The Savage Heart: A Conversation with Eric Hoffer."

84. Hoffer, *The Temper of Our Time*, 41–57.

85. Eric Hoffer, "Negro Must Be His Own Ancestor," *Los Angeles Times*, December 28, 1969, H9.

86. CBS News, "The Savage Heart: A Conversation with Eric Hoffer."

87. For documentation on CBS paying Hoffer for interviews, see David Klinger, letter to Eric Hoffer, May 7, 1969 (Eric Hoffer Papers, Hoover Archives, Box 65); Cass Canfield, letter to Eric Hoffer, April 11, 1968 (Eric Hoffer Papers, Hoover Archives, Box 30); Cass Canfield, letter to Eric Hoffer, April 26, 1968 (Eric Hoffer Papers, Hoover Archives, Box 30).

88. "People," *Time*, March 2, 1970, 42.

89. Hoffer's negative characterization of Ronald Reagan can be found in his interview with Eric Sevareid. CBS News, "Eric Hoffer: The Passionate State of Mind."

90. CBS News, "The Savage Heart: A Conversation with Eric Hoffer."

91. Hoffer, *Before the Sabbath*, 116.

92. Robert Kirsch, "Eric Hoffer's Conversations Reveal Pattern of Concern," *Los Angeles Times*, February 11, 1969, D6.

93. Hoffer, *Before the Sabbath*, 19.

Chapter 5
Poet of the Pulps

1. Al Kuettner, "Eric Hoffer: 'She Told Me I Would Die at 40. . . . Now I Am Like a Tourist on This Earth,'" *Chicago Tribune*, January 28, 1968, J23.

2. Ray Bradbury, "The Murderer," in *Classic Stories I* (New York: Bantam, 1990), 55.

3. Sam Weller, *Listen to the Echoes: The Ray Bradbury Interviews* (Chicago: Stop Smiling Books, 2010), 27–28.

4. Sam Weller, *The Bradbury Chronicles: The Life of Ray Bradbury* (New York: William Morrow, 2005), 12, 30, 55–56, 87, 120.

5. Quoted in Weller, *The Bradbury Chronicles*, 85.

6. Ray Bradbury, e-mail interview with author, September 25–27, 2010. Because Ray Bradbury famously eschews such modern contrivances as e-mail, the discussion took place through the intermediary of Ray's daughter, Alexandra.

7. Ray Bradbury, "To the Chicago Abyss," in *The Machineries of Joy* (New York: Bantam, 1965), 199.

8. Weller, *The Bradbury Chronicles*, 69, 80, 82, 89.

9. Ibid., 102.

10. Ibid., 65–66, 69–76.

11. Ibid., 144, 239.

12. Ray Bradbury, "Banshee," in *The Toynbee Convector* (New York: Bantam, 1989), 96–108. The author's Ahab-like obsession with Huston found book-length expression in Ray Bradbury, *Green Shadows, White Whale* (New York: Knopf, 1992).

13. Jonathan R. Eller and William Touponce, *Ray Bradbury: The Life of Fiction* (Kent, OH: Kent State University Press, 2004), 286.

14. Weller, *Listen to the Echoes*, 59–63; Weller, *The Bradbury Chronicles*, 253–55.

15. "'Fahrenheit 451' Author Wants Title Back," MSNBC, June 29, 2004, http://www.msnbc.msn.com/id/5324876/, accessed July 28, 2010; "Ray Bradbury Rips Michael Moore," *WorldNetDaily*, June 3, 2004, http://www.wnd.com/?pageId=24908, accessed July 28, 2010.

16. Weller, *The Bradbury Chronicles*, 289.

17. *Molle Mystery Theater*, "Killer, Come Back to Me," NBC (radio), May 17, 1946.

18. Weller, *The Bradbury Chronicles*, 143.

19. *X Minus One*, "The Veldt," NBC (radio), August 4, 1955; Ray Bradbury, "The Veldt," in *The Illustrated Man* (Garden City, NY: Doubleday, 1951), 15–29.

20. *Suspense*, "The Crowd," CBS (radio), September 21, 1950; Ray Bradbury, "The Crowd," in *The October Country* (New York: Ballantine, 1955, 1967), 145–55.

21. Quoted in Weller, *The Bradbury Chronicles*, 261.

22. Weller, *Listen to the Echoes*, 64–65; Weller, *The Bradbury Chronicles*, 237–38.

23. Bradbury, e-mail interview with author, September 25–27, 2010.

24. Weller, *The Bradbury Chronicles*, 171–72.

25. Eller and Touponce, *Ray Bradbury*, 2.

26. Ibid., 61–62, 159–60.

27. Ibid., 160, 359, 362, 370.

28. Weller, *The Bradbury Chronicles*, 124–25.

29. "Poet of the Pulps," *Time*, March 23, 1953, 114.

30. Ray Bradbury, "I See You Never," *Classic Stories I*, 68–71.

31. Quoted in Weller, *The Bradbury Chronicles*, 188.

32. Ray Bradbury, "The Big Black and White Game," in *Classic Stories I*, 77–88; Ray Bradbury, "The Other Foot," in *The Illustrated Man*, 43–57.

33. Ray Bradbury, "The Day It Rained Forever," in *A Medicine for Melancholy* (New York: Perennial, 1960, 2001), 118–28.

34. Russell Kirk, "The World of Ray Bradbury," in *Enemies of the Permanent Things* (New Rochelle, NY: Arlington House, 1969), 116.

35. Quoted in James Hibberd, "Ray Bradbury Is on Fire!," *Salon*, August 29, 2001, http://www.salon.com/people/feature/2001/08/29/bradbury/print.html, accessed May 5, 2010.

36. Jennifer Steinhauer, "At 88, a Writer Fights for Libraries, and Tells a Few of Life's Tales," *New York Times*, June 20, 2009, A12.

37. Ray Bradbury, *Dandelion Wine* (New York: Bantam Books, 1957, 1976), 33, 53–63.

38. Ibid., 80–87.

39. Ray Bradbury, "The Rocket," in *Classic Stories I*, 182–92.

40. Ray Bradbury, "The Machineries of Joy," in *The Machineries of Joy*, p. 1.

41. Ray Bradbury, "I Sing the Body Electric," in *I Sing the Body Electric and Other Stories* (New York: Perennial, 2001), 137.

42. Bradbury, "The Murderer," 55.

43. Ray Bradbury, "Almost the End of the World," in *The Machineries of Joy*, 63–70.

44. Bradbury, "The Murderer," 53–61.

45. Bradbury, "The Veldt," 15–29.

46. Weller, *Listen to the Echoes*, 255.

47. Quoted in Hibberd, "Ray Bradbury Is on Fire!"

48. Bradbury, "The Crowd," 145–55.

49. Weller, *The Bradbury Chronicles*, 278–79.

50. Ibid., 3.

51. Bradbury, *The Martian Chronicles*, 32–48.

52. Ray Bradbury, "Just This Side of Byzantium," in *Dandelion Wine*, viii–ix.

53. Ray Bradbury, *Fahrenheit 451* (1953; repr. New York: Ballantine Books, 1982), 59.

54. Ibid., 96–97.

55. Ray Bradbury, "Afterword," in ibid., 167–68.

56. Eller and Touponce, *Ray Bradbury*, 181, 185.

57. Steinhauer, "At 88, a Writer Fights for Libraries, and Tells a Few of Life's Tales," A1.

58. Eller and Touponce, *Ray Bradbury*, 443–81.

59. Bradbury, e-mail interview with author, September 25–27, 2010.

60. Eller and Touponce, *Ray Bradbury*, 453.

61. Bradbury, "The Murderer," 59.

62. Susan King, "Ray Bradbury Hates Big Government: 'Our Country Is in Need of a Revolution,'" *Los Angeles Times*, August 16, 2010, http://latimesblogs.latimes.com/herocomplex/2010/08/ray-bradbury-is-sick-of-big-government-our-country-is-in-need-of-a-revolution-/.html, accessed August 16, 2010.

63. Quoted in Hibberd, "Ray Bradbury Is on Fire!"

64. Ray Bradbury, "Long Division," in *The Toynbee Convector*, 176–80.

65. Ray Bradbury, "The Exiles," in *Classic Stories I*, 234–48.

Acknowledgments

Writing Blue Collar Intellectuals was a white-collar endeavor. I spent a great deal of time researching in archives. This white-collar work included trips to the University of Chicago and Syracuse University to comb through Mortimer Adler's papers; to the Hoover Archives on the Stanford University campus to research Milton Friedman; and to the San Francisco Public Library and the Hoover Archives to get to know the unknowable Eric Hoffer. So many librarians, whose names and faces have meshed together with the passage of time, deserve my thanks. Since I can't thank them all specifically, I give thanks to their profession.

I assure you that all of this white-collar work was done in a very blue-collar way. Unable to afford lodging, I camped out on one of the many lakes in upstate New York when I examined boxes of Adler materials at Syracuse. I thank my family for enduring that journey that yielded one endnote. I piggybacked further Adler research at the University of Chicago upon a talk at DePaul. Young America's Foundation's Pat Coyle has my appreciation for booking that lecture so convenient in time and location. I am especially grateful to Karl and Jane Anderson, who let me crash when I researched at Hoover and the San Francisco Public Library. Staying in one of the most expensive destinations in America for a couple of weeks simply wouldn't have been possible without their opening up their home.

John J. Miller encouraged me to write a piece on the Durants for *National Review*, which really got the gears turning in my head for a book exploring some of the themes I initially addressed in that article. Jed Donahue believed in the book and did a wonderful job editing it. Lili Osborne, who in the final of her nearly ninety-four years shared several hours with me, gave me a conversation I will remember for the rest of my years.

I wish I could say a beneficent foundation or a kindly millionaire bankrolled the activities that bankrupted me. I can't. But I can say that many good-hearted individuals, named and unnamed, made my work possible. People are great.

I suppose I enjoyed writing *Blue Collar Intellectuals* so much because I can relate. Subjects for earlier books interested me because they were so alien; these half-dozen blue-collar intellectuals interested me because we shared much in common—and because the combination of my background and interests makes me feel a bit of an alien. Before I became an author, I delivered the *Boston Globe* for five years, worked at Fenway Park for seven, profited as an occasional high-school ticket scalper and keg-race organizer, and served in the Marines. That earlier life was followed by an adult life consumed by reading and writing. What had been a hobby became a vocation.

I identify with my subjects. I believe the average reader will more readily identify with them, too. People from ordinary backgrounds are capable of extraordinary accomplishments. The Durants, Adler, Hoffer, Friedman, and Bradbury prove this.

Index